MW01063169

THE SHONEN JUMP GUIDE TO MAKING MANGA

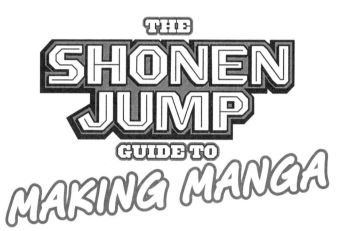

THE
SHONEN JUMP
GUIDE TO
MAKING MANGA

Weekly Shonen Jump
Editorial Department

VIZ MEDIA

THE SHONEN JUMP GUIDE TO MAKING MANGA
Shonen Jump Edition

VIZ MEDIA EDITION
Translation: Caleb Cook
Lettering: Brandon Bovia
Design: Francesca Truman
Editor: David Brothers

JAPANESE EDITION
Planning/Editing: *Weekly Shonen Jump* Editorial Department, Yu Saito
Illustration: mato
Composition: Ichishi Iida
Design/Layout: Takehiko Ishiyama [FREIHEIT]
Editor: Hiroyuki Nakano

Printed in Canada

Published by VIZ Media, LLC
P.O. Box 77010 | San Francisco, CA 94107

Library of Congress Control Number: 2022936879

10 9 8 7 6 5 4 3 2 1
First printing, October 2022

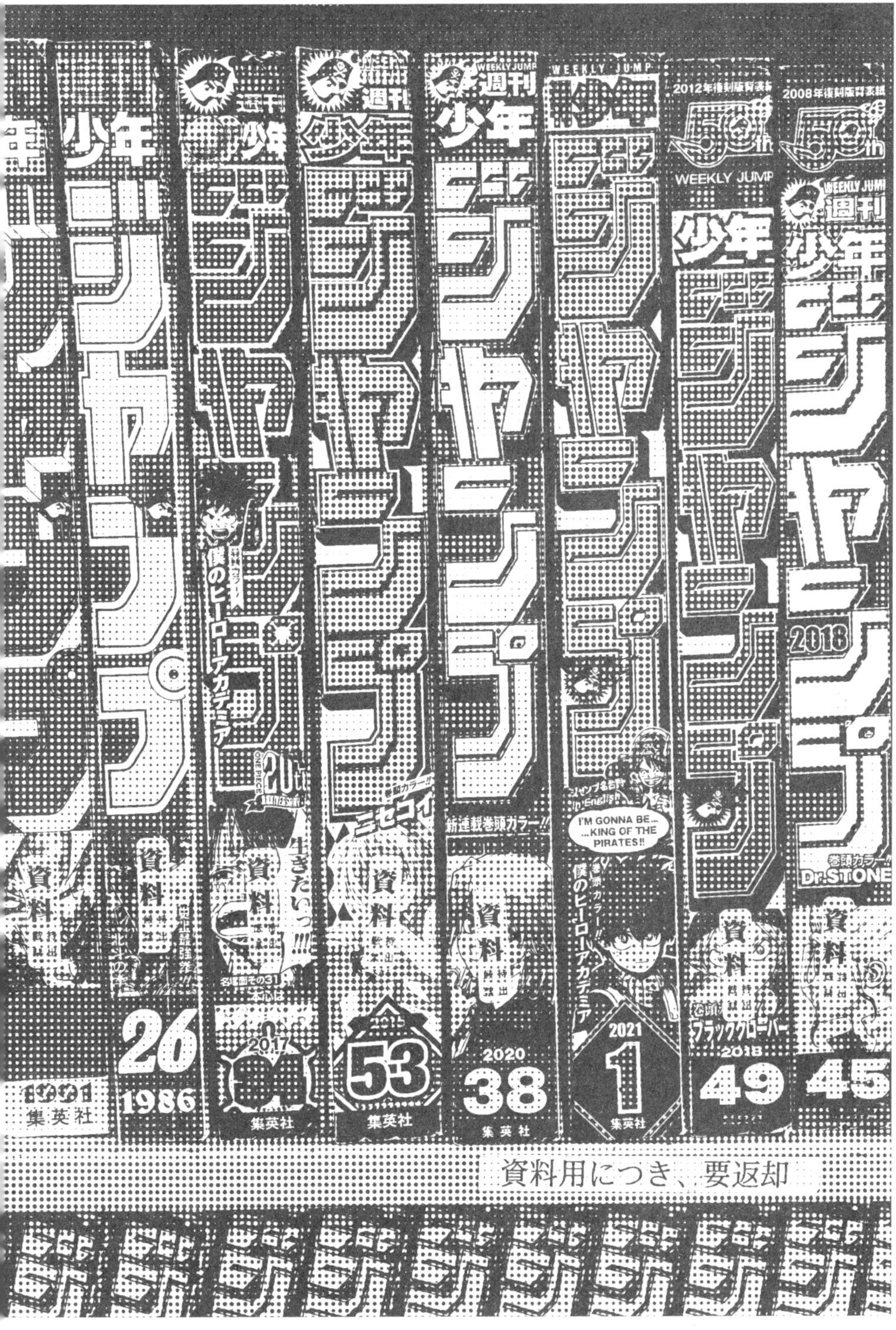
1986
26
集英社
週刊
少年ジャンプ
僕のヒーローアカデミア
ONE PIECE 20th ANNIVERSARY
2017
集英社
WEEKLY JUMP
週刊
少年ジャンプ
ニセコイ
53
集英社
WEEKLY JUMP
週刊
少年ジャンプ
新連載巻頭カラー!!
2020
38
集英社
WEEKLY JUMP
少年ジャンプ
I'M GONNA BE... ...KING OF THE PIRATES!!
巻頭カラー
僕のヒーローアカデミア
2021
1
PIRATES
集英社
2012年復刻版背表紙
50th
WEEKLY JUMP
少年ジャンプ
ブラッククローバー
2018
49
2008年復刻版背表紙
50th
WEEKLY JUMP
週刊
少年ジャンプ
2018
巻頭カラー!!
Dr.STONE
45
資料
資料用につき、要返却

THE SHONEN JUMP GUIDE TO MAKING MANGA
—————— TABLE OF CONTENTS ——————

1

READ THIS WAY

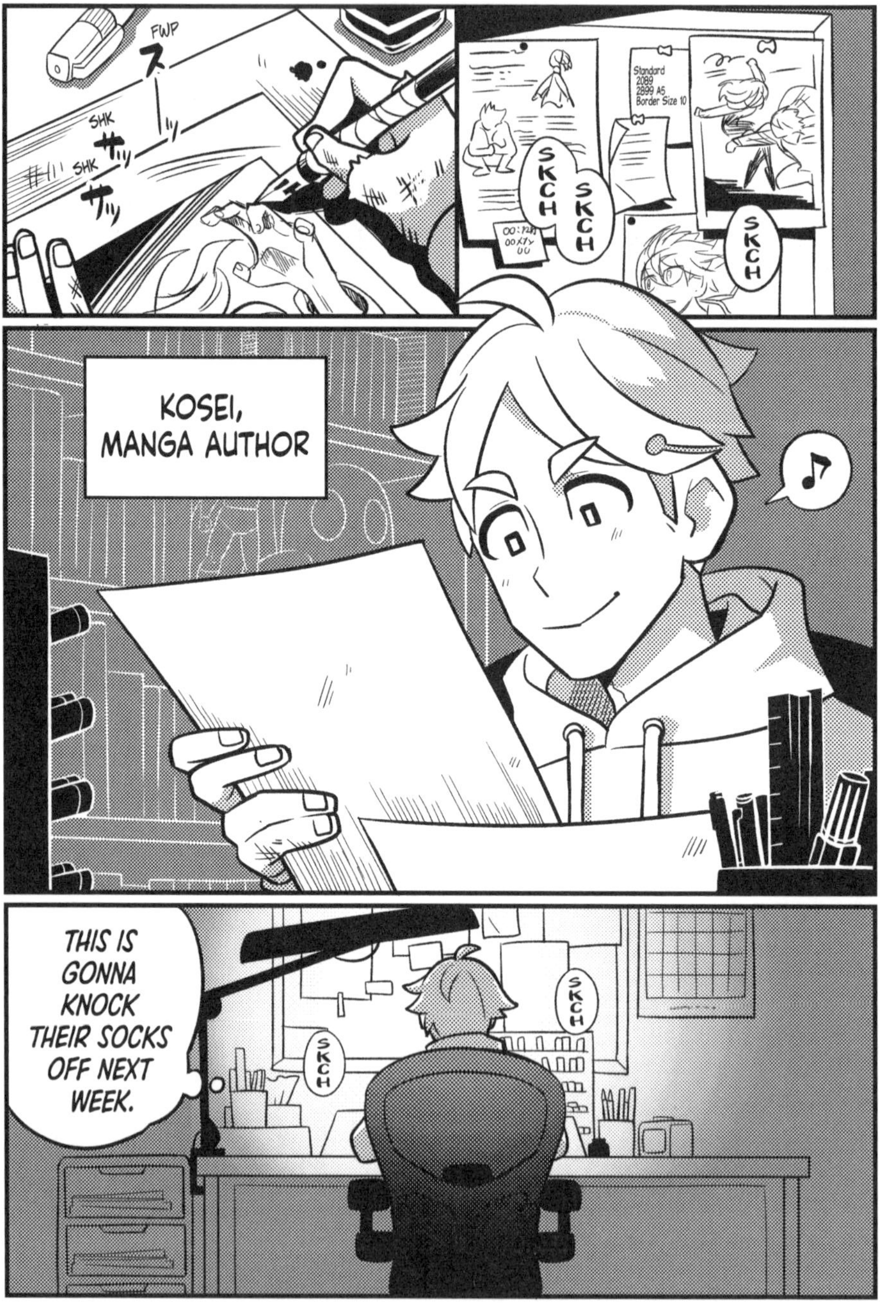

Standard
2089
2899 A5
Border Size 10
SKCH
SKCH
SKCH
FWP
SHK
SHK
KOSEI, MANGA AUTHOR
♪
SKCH
SKCH
THIS IS GONNA KNOCK THEIR SOCKS OFF NEXT WEEK.

SENSEI! I THINK I FINALLY GET HOW SUZU'S POWER WORKS!

YUP.

YES! SOME PEOPLE SAW THIS TWIST COMING!

KOSEI'S ASSISTANTS

DID I FIGURE IT OUT? IS THAT HOW IT WORKS? YOU GOTTA TELL ME, SENSEI!

SHAKA

SHAKA

Sigh...

THIS IS ACTUALLY AMAZING...

KOSEI SENSEI WAS **BORN** TO CREATE MANGA.

IS HE EVER *NOT* JUST HAVING A TOTAL BLAST?

STILL A SECRET, FOR NOW...

3

READ THIS WAY

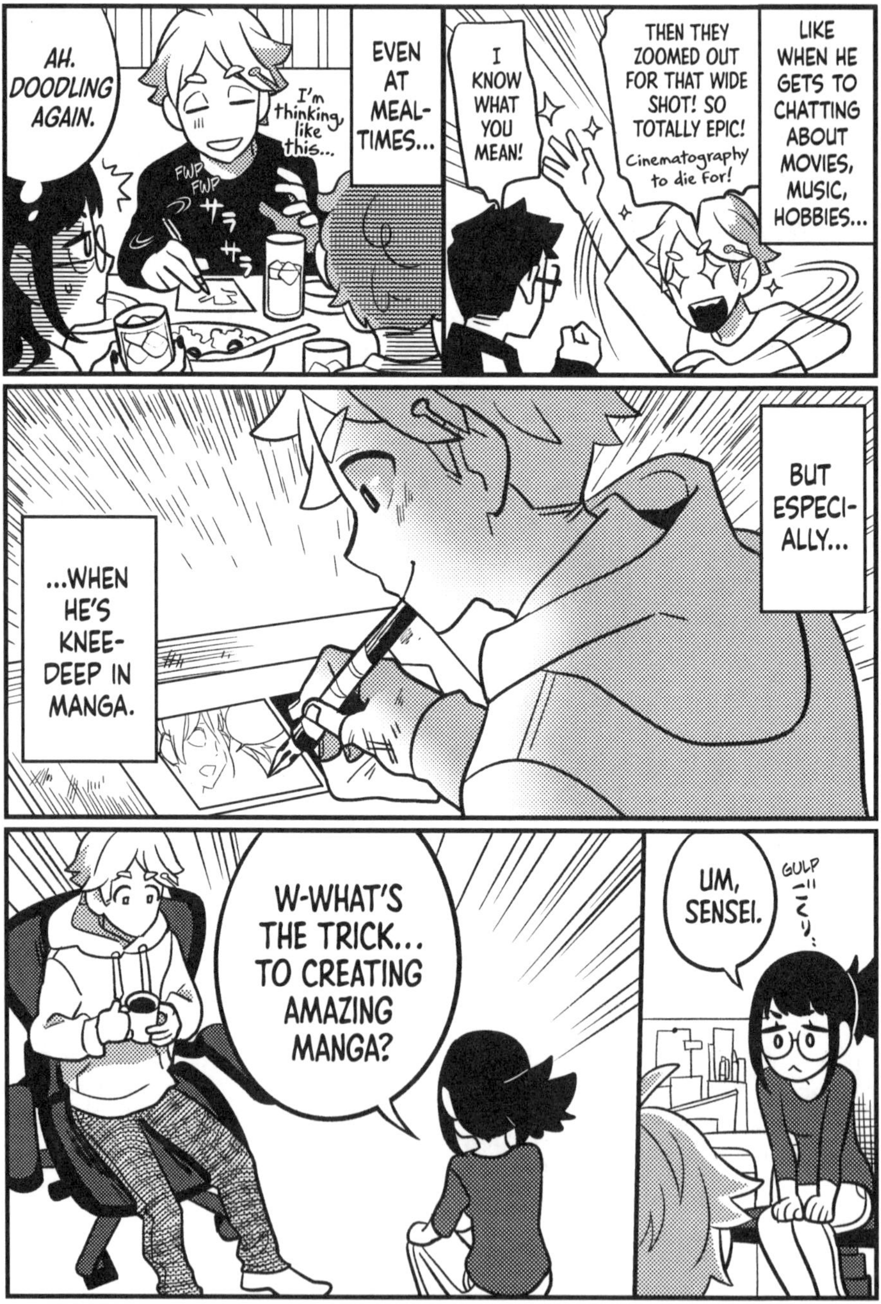
LIKE WHEN HE GETS TO CHATTING ABOUT MOVIES, MUSIC, HOBBIES...
THEN THEY ZOOMED OUT FOR THAT WIDE SHOT! SO TOTALLY EPIC!
Cinematography to die for!
I KNOW WHAT YOU MEAN!
EVEN AT MEAL-TIMES...
I'm thinking, like this...
FWP FWP
AH. DOODLING AGAIN.
BUT ESPECI-ALLY...
...WHEN HE'S KNEE-DEEP IN MANGA.
UM, SENSEI.
GULP
W-WHAT'S THE TRICK... TO CREATING AMAZING MANGA?

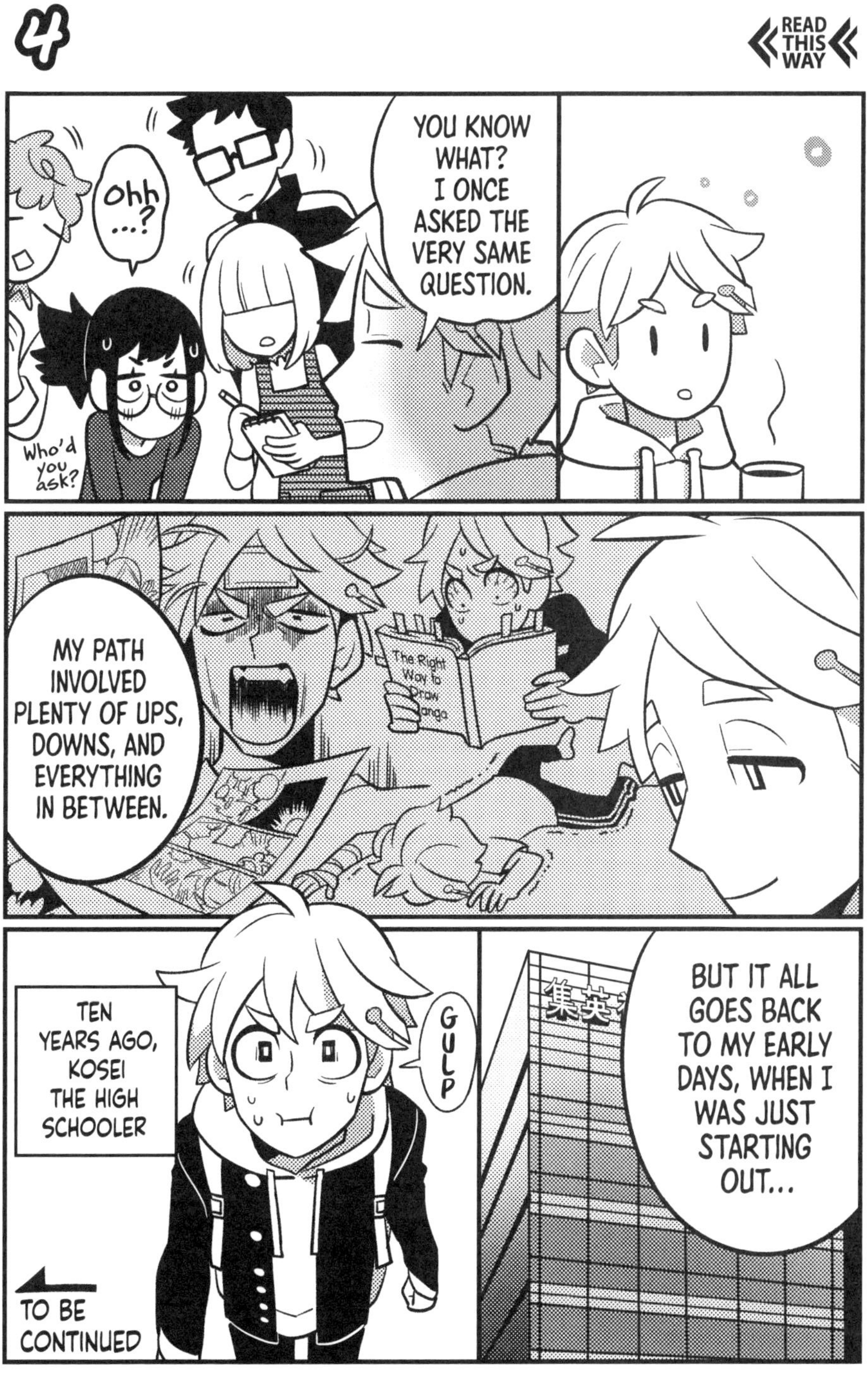
4
READ THIS WAY
YOU KNOW WHAT? I ONCE ASKED THE VERY SAME QUESTION.
Ohh ...?
Who'd you ask?
MY PATH INVOLVED PLENTY OF UPS, DOWNS, AND EVERYTHING IN BETWEEN.
The Right Way to Draw
BUT IT ALL GOES BACK TO MY EARLY DAYS, WHEN I WAS JUST STARTING OUT...
集英
GULP
TEN YEARS AGO, KOSEI THE HIGH SCHOOLER
TO BE CONTINUED

GETTING GOING

Perhaps you want to create manga, but you're not sure where to start? Or maybe you've already begun, but you're curious if you're going about it the right way? This book was made for people with those kinds of concerns, whether they're complete beginners or budding manga authors on the verge of their professional debut. Within these pages, we, the *Weekly Shonen Jump* editorial staff, will do our best to explain how to lower some of the hurdles present when creating manga, and how to keep the work fun and exciting.

Maybe you're thinking, "That just sounds like a rule book for manga." Well, you're not entirely wrong. The original concept for this book had more of a "how to draw easy-to-read manga" approach, which would've provided technical breakdowns on page and panel layout, and other such things. After talking it over with several *Jump* manga authors, their feedback was mostly along the lines of, "Emphasizing technical know-how is a surefire way to bog down readers with a bunch of preconceived notions, which could then paralyze them when it comes time to sit down and draw."

Mastering any sort of skill requires training your mind and body. On one side you have knowledge and mental processes, and on the other you have muscle memory that comes from drawing. Those are two pillars. But at the end of the day, it's the spirit that drives both mind and body forward. By placing disproportionate importance on the minutiae of knowledge and technique, we might accidentally kill off that essential, driving element, which is an author's desire to create whatever they like, however they like. In essence, you risk putting the cart before the horse.

What we ought to be doing is lighting fires of inspiration that make readers say, "This is the kind of thing I'm into" and "This is what I want to draw" and "This is what I'm capable of drawing." That may sound like idealistic fluff, but we truly believe the most important thing when it comes to making manga is that spirit that encourages you to pick up the pencil and draw what you want within your abilities. The way we see it, that's no empty platitude.

The world at large has plenty of instructional texts, articles, and web videos on how to write and how to create art. Nevertheless, the pros themselves say that "more important than skills and technique is the mental groundwork" and "being paralyzed by all the technical know-how is a great way to kill off the desire to create anything at all."

Whether you're a total newcomer or someone with real experience under their belt, we hope this book proves useful at times when you're at a dead end, searching for the "correct" way to make manga; when fear of failure halts your progress; or when you're just in a creative slump. But beyond methods to inspire you and keep up your motivation (that being the "spirit" side of things), we've also included a bit about techniques and skills (the "mind" and "body" side) that should be helpful to aspiring manga authors. We've surveyed a number of *Jump* authors about the process leading to their debuts, and there are other chapters about choosing digital creation products and picking out analog art tools.

Needless to say, a single book can't possibly cover every technique breakdown or practice method on the road to becoming a manga author. These pages contain what we feel are the most important points, but it's by no means an exhaustive overview. If you're a beginner who manages to take those first few steps, eventually speaking with an editor about your work's strengths and weaknesses can help fill in those knowledge gaps.

If nothing else, the takeaway from this book should be, "Pack what you love into your work!"

All else will flow from there.

INTRODUCING THE CHARACTERS

KOSEI
A 15-YEAR-OLD WHO DREAMS OF MAKING MANGA, THOUGH HE HASN'T CREATED A SINGLE SERIES YET.

SAITO
THE MANGA EDITOR WHO TAKES A LOOK AT KOSEI'S SAMPLE. THEY SAY HIS BOOKSHELVES AT HOME ONCE COLLAPSED UNDER THE WEIGHT OF TOO MUCH MANGA.

ASADA
LEGENDARY MANGA EDITOR AND SAITO'S BOSS. HE'S SO PASSIONATE AND KNOWLEDGE-ABLE ABOUT MANGA THAT PEOPLE WONDER IF HE'S SOME SORT OF MANGA DEITY INCARNATE.

PRELUDE TO CREATION — HOW TO BEGIN

This chapter depicts a series of meetings between *Jump* editor Saito and first-year high school student Kosei, a manga author in the making who one day brought his art sample to the *Weekly Shonen Jump* publisher Shueisha, a common occurence for aspiring manga creators in Japan. Saito will be explaining to Kosei how one could go about learning to create manga, starting from square one.

But long before diving into the intricacies of how to draw manga, every potential author first needs to look within and ask themselves what sort of manga they *want* to create. Nothing is more essential.

What do we mean by this, exactly?

▓ How do I know where to start?

AS-YET-UNNAMED BOY: Hello, my name is Kosei Mochida, I'm fifteen years old, and this is the first time I've ever brought in a sample for review. Please take a look, if you don't mind!

SAITO: I'm Saito, a member of Shueisha's *Weekly Shonen Jump* editorial department. Thanks for coming in today. Well, no time to lose—let me see what you've brought us. Hmm. Hmm? This isn't manga... It's a single page of character drawings. And you haven't even inked them yet, eh?

KOSEI: "Inked"? I'm not sure what that means.

SAITO: First off, making manga requires something called a **storyboard**. It's essentially a very rough draft, but still one that includes a plot and page layouts. From there, you create the **underdrawing** with pencil on proper draft paper. The next and final version would be the **inks**, which is done with G-pens and mapping nibs, and all the finishing touches as well. I'm describing an analog process, of course, though these days plenty of people opt for a digital method instead. You'll find much more detailed explanations on the internet, or in any number of books. That is certainly recommended reading.

KOSEI: Man, I had no idea. I'll check those out for sure!

SAITO: As the *manga* editorial department, we can't do much with your single page of illustrations, but tell me—were you really hoping to make it big as an *illustrator*, facing down the world with your one page of drawings? Or do you want to be a manga author, and create stories in a comic format?

KOSEI: Uh, the second one! Manga author! The problem is, all that business about writing a story? And breaking pages down into panels? There's so much do when it comes to manga, that I dunno where to start. But there's gotta be a "right" way to create manga, right? To be honest, I'm convinced that *Jump* editors must have some secret, legendary manga textbook locked in a safe that could help anyone learn to do it like the pros. I'd love to take a peek!

SAITO: I see, I see... Yes, starting out can be tricky. Sadly, there is no secret *Jump* textbook, though you're not the first one to ask about such a thing. **There's no resource that can teach you the "correct" way to make manga.** In fact, you're misleading yourself if you think that a singular correct method exists at all.

KOSEI: Darn... So you can't really give me any advice?

SAITO: As professionals, of course we know about the techniques involved, but there's so much more to it than that...

◼ I don't have a solid idea to work on yet, but I'd like to learn about creating characters and stories.

KOSEI: Sure! Like, could you tell me how to come up with awesome characters, stories, and worlds?

SAITO: That's not necessarily something that can be taught. Especially if you yourself don't have a clear picture of what it is you want to do just yet. Once that goal is in place, I'd be happy to give you more concrete tips.

KOSEI: So those tips are off-limits until I've come up with my goal, or ending?

SAITO: I'm afraid there's no magic formula for conceiving great ideas for manga characters and plots. **There is no single methodology that applies to every author and every story.** Sure, you'll find books, articles, and interviews that provide hints, and any good editor could tell you other works to reference in relation to your own, but no—**there's no secret formula with the steps for creating an awesome manga.** Besides, if you dip into all that knowledge floating out there before conceptualizing what it is you want to achieve, you could end up bogged down and unable to progress.

KOSEI: I think I get it. You'll be able to tell me more once I bring you an actual manga I've created?

SAITO: Exactly. Each author has to really grapple with whichever series they're working on at the moment to even begin to pin down that series' fun factor. That factor is something born deep within you, so you'll have to dig deep and ask yourself questions like, "What am I into?" or "What is it I want to do?" That has to be the first step.

KOSEI: Got it. Is there anything at all you can teach me now, at the stage I'm at?

SAITO: Considering you've never created a manga before, we'll have to start with the most basic of training tips and the frame of mind you'll need.

■ What's an effective way to practice? Is there a short route to creating manga?

KOSEI: All right, say that I'm just not good enough yet to come up with a bunch of characters and story lines. Should I start by studying the techniques themselves? Like how to draw in the first place, or how to break up a page into panels?

SAITO: But you haven't created any actual manga yet, right, Kosei?

KOSEI: Right, which is why I wanna learn all those techniques. Then everything else will fall into place and I'll be drawing in no time.

SAITO: Hmm. How do I put this... Tell me, Kosei, are you right-handed?

KOSEI: Uhh, yup. Sure am. What, do lefties have a better chance of making it as pro manga authors, or something?

SAITO: No, nothing like that. Just bear with me for a moment. As a righty, you probably don't write very well with your left hand, yes? But imagine that one day, you were suddenly forced to use your left hand. Would you go around doing research and asking people the ins and out of writing the alphabet?

KOSEI: Nope! I'd just practice over and over until my left hand got the hang of it.

SAITO: Precisely. It's the same way with manga. You have to practice until it becomes a skill you can call your own.

KOSEI: So, what's the most effective way to practice? What's a reliable route to becoming a manga author?

SAITO: Draw what you love. Draw what you're capable of drawing. That's the quickest way to go about it. Only start worrying about the techniques and technicalities later on, when they'll actually serve you. No matter what stage an author is at, they're best off starting by identifying their own likes and interests.

KOSEI: Okay, and how do I go about doing that?

SAITO: The very first thing would be to **talk with other people** about manga series you love and ones you're not so fond of. Family, friends, editors—whomever. Through that process, you'll slowly gain the ability to approach these works critically, analyze them, and put your feelings about them into words. My next suggestion would be **to copy, by hand, some of your favorite manga**. Not just the characters, but entire scenes, across several pages or even a whole chapter. Be sure to include the paneling, the backgrounds, and even the word balloons.

KOSEI: Just straight-up copying, you mean? I thought tracing is always frowned upon...

SAITO: Of course, doing that for a contest or official submission without express permission would get you in trouble. I'm just talking about a way to practice and learn how a given manga is put together on the most basic level. It can show you how an author approaches every page of their story with intention, and how they utilize specific elements in deliberate ways. Why did they arrange the panels on the page in just such a way? Why was a word balloon placed in one spot or another? Why did they include a close-up

of the character at this particular point? Why have hand lettering here, versus somewhere else? And so on and so forth. As you copy the manga, consider what the most important element is in any given panel. Try to imagine the author's intent. Or, to put it another way, you won't learn a thing through mindless copying without analysis. **Once you're done copying, compare your version to the original with a fine-tooth comb.** What are the key differences? What did you overlook, and why? Say that your attempt to reproduce an impactful character expression somehow falls flat. Ask yourself why. Are the eyebrows in the wrong spot? Is the angle of the smile just a little bit off? Are the eyes wonky? That sort of thing.

■ Why should I copy my favorite series?

KOSEI: We're talking about my favorite series, right? I've already read them over and over, so why do I have to redraw them?

SAITO: Based on experience, many of the best authors out there tend to say, "Look, and draw what you see." It's remarkably hard to improve just by trying to draw what you can picture in your own mind. In other words, reading manga isn't enough, because there's so much more you'll start to realize once you attempt to draw it yourself. Great manga doesn't emerge that way purely by happenstance or dumb luck. Where should each character be placed? Which faces deserve the close-up? The author considers all of these questions as they draw. You're a million times more able to tune in to the author's creativity by reproducing their work, as opposed to just reading it. Ah, and don't forget to copy the dialogue as well. You'll come to understand the proper amount of text to include in a word balloon, where in the panel the dialogue should be placed, and what sort of speech rhythms are pleasing to your own ear.

KOSEI: Makes sense... It's like experiencing the pro author's work vicariously!

SAITO: While you're at it, expand beyond manga and **sketch what interests you out in the world** as well. You can expand your metaphorical art library by drawing real-life people, scenery, buildings, and so on. Even if your goal is to draw fantasy worlds, sketches of real places can help with that. Think about the various islands in *One Piece*, which might have motifs based on the ancient Roman Colosseum, or the canal-lined city of Venice. Meanwhile, *Demon Slayer: Kimetsu no Yaiba* is set in Taisho-era Japan, while *Burn the Witch* takes place in England. You'll find those sorts of inspirations being used in any number of famous, fantastical, fictional stories. By incorporating real-life scenery and architecture into your work, you'll achieve a sense of world building that goes beyond the all-too-common "vaguely medieval fantasy world." Narrowing down a time period and location also makes it much easier to collect reference materials.

KOSEI: I kinda get the impression that a lot of these authors tend to have an interest in the stuff they're referencing!

SAITO: I have to agree. That's just one more reason why it's important to nail down what it is that you specifically like.

KOSEI: Can you elaborate a little? I'm still not totally clear why that's so important.

▉ What's the point of all this stuff?

SAITO: You're asking why that introspection is so necessary? Why you should dig down to figure out what you like? Well, if we pare down manga creation into its two most basic steps, they would be: 1) **pick what you want to draw**, and 2) **break it all down into pages and panels**. Without actual subject matter to work with, what good will it do you to know drawing techniques? That's why coming up with your material comes first.

KOSEI: But does my own manga have to be based around my own likes and interests? My goal is to create a series that does new, cool stuff that screams "originality," and I feel like a manga with really clear influences is bound to get slammed as a rip-off.

SAITO: Plagiarizing is wrong, of course. You can't just copy someone else's character designs, writing, photos, or drawings. But the work of

any creator—no matter who they are—is fundamentally **a melting pot that blends their interests and influences**.

KOSEI: Like a bunch of ingredients from different sources, tossed in together and mixed around?

SAITO: Take Masashi Kishimoto Sensei, for instance. You probably think of Naruto as a completely original work, right?

KOSEI: Well, duh! It never would've gotten that popular around the world if it were some kind of rip-off.

SAITO: Well, in interviews, Kishimoto Sensei has cited a number of influences, including manga like *Dragon Ball*, *Blade of the Immortal*, and *Akira*, as well as the works of Production I.G. on the anime side. But when you're reading it, *Naruto* probably doesn't feel like a rip-off of those other properties, right? Every creator has influences that wind up blending with their own life experiences and ways of thinking. As long as you're not consciously creating an homage to something, **your own quirks are sure to shine through**.

◼ How do I create original works after copying so much?

KOSEI: I see... So that explains how a melting pot made of my faves won't necessarily come across as a rip-off, but I'm still kinda curious about why my work *should* start with stuff I like.

SAITO: It's good to know you're paying attention, but don't get ahead of yourself! In any case, there are two reasons, and the first has to do with motivation. Simply put, **drawing what you like is a way to keep the work fun and interesting**. Those who haven't created manga can't possibly imagine just how taxing the work really is, both physically and mentally. The struggle would become unbearable if, on top of everything, an author had to draw something that didn't interest them in the least. Meanwhile, **drawing pages upon pages of what you actually like** is the best way to improve as a manga author. When enjoyment is the motivation to pick up the pen, the rest will follow, which is why the works you admire should be sources of inspiration. So don't stop after copying one of your favorite series—keep going with several others as well.

KOSEI: That's one reason to use stuff I like for the soup base in my melting pot. What's the second?

SAITO: To discover your own particular flavor and individuality. The characteristics and specialties of *your* work. Basically, the "originality" factor you brought up. How else would you come to realize such things?

KOSEI: Uhh, I'm imagining, like, this sudden, epic awakening that just happens outta the blue one day. My eyes would glow with a big burst of light. That kind of thing.

SAITO: Hah, everyone's lives would be easier if it worked that way. The real answer, though, is taste. At some point while drawing what you love, your own habits will start to emerge.

As you copy your favorite series, you'll find yourself coming to realizations like, "This one ultimate attack makes for an awesome scene!" or "This character is the coolest ever" or "I wish I could draw facial expressions like this one" or "I love it when the guy builds up so much rage and then it all explodes out" or even "What I really want to draw is cute girls." **All of that builds to form your sense of taste** and provides hints about what you want to draw and what your particular style will be known for.

KOSEI: But is it really enough to only focus on what I already like?

SAITO: Hmm! Why would you doubt that?

◼ Will my manga sell even if my tastes are strange?

KOSEI: But if what I'm into isn't that trendy, my manga probably won't sell, right?

SAITO: Don't pay any mind to trends.

KOSEI: For real?

SAITO: I mean it—that shouldn't matter. Say you genuinely like the big, trendy series. Say they make your heart cry out, "This is *amazing*!" Then you should absolutely go ahead and treat those series as ones worth emulating. On the flip side, say you can't figure out what's so appealing about the trendy best sellers, but despite that, you say to yourself, "This is what's popular, so that's the sort of content I'll cram into my work." That sort of shallow, surface-level pandering won't produce anything worthwhile that lasts. Even the act of drawing with that mindset will take its toll on you.

KOSEI: I always thought you have to give the public exactly what they want if you're hoping to sell books...

SAITO: From everything I've observed, the big hits aren't made by authors who jump on the bandwagon. They come from authors whose clear message is, "***This* is what I want to show the world**!" When I do come across a creator who's remarkably skilled at incorporating trendy elements into their work, I get the feeling they genuinely enjoy that popular stuff anyway, deep down.

◼ Does creating manga require you to know about sales numbers and stuff?

KOSEI: Seriously? I always thought that some of the big hits had to be products of paying close attention to sales, performance, metrics... All that sort of technical feedback. Can you explain that stuff?

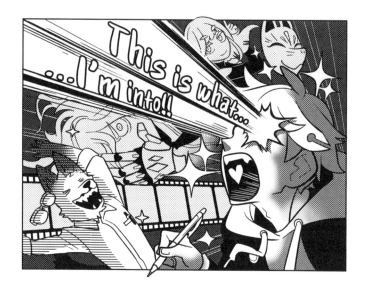

SAITO: What you're describing sounds like taking customer feedback and using it to craft the ideal product for that audience. Here at *Jump*, we do value the weekly reader surveys, but they hardly steer the ship. Once a manga has been serialized, our job is to help the author match what they want to create with what the audience wants to read. Without that inner desire to create, all the data and trends in the world wouldn't be enough to produce quality manga. **There's no greater weapon in this war than knowing what you like and what you want to draw**.

KOSEI: I dunno... Are you sure about that?

SAITO: I realize how it comes off, but I assure you this is all coming from my lived experience.

KOSEI: Well, what if I told you that a lot of my faves don't run in *Jump*, but in the more minor magazines? Is it really a good idea for me to focus my energy on understanding those series?

SAITO: Your particular interests come together to form another unique weapon in your arsenal, which is a good thing. That said, if one of your goals is achieving a large readership, then you will have to **consider how to use your art and your themes creatively to attract a wider audience**. That can be a separate matter from knowing where your own interests lie. If you lose sight of that original spark, you won't reach a single soul. Authors hoping to be serialized in *Jump* will often produce a number of one-shot stories, carefully consider reader feedback, and fine-tune their work until it appeals to more and more readers.

KOSEI: I guess so! I know there are lots of authors who thought their particular brand just wasn't right for *Jump* based on how their one-shots did, but then, once they made it into the magazine with a serialization, they got really popular anyway. That's kinda what you mean, huh?

■ Are there cases where a manga author just doesn't jibe with *Jump* or with a given editor?

SAITO: Of course, an author's particularities do have to jibe with the *Jump* brand. Some will meet with disappointment when they bring their samples to us, yet go on to find success elsewhere. Others might make their debuts in other magazines first, before making it big in *Jump*. The person has to mesh with the magazine, but there's certainly more to a series' value than just its popularity. Sadly, I've known plenty of cases where a newcomer didn't harmonize with a particular editor or department, became convinced that they weren't cut out for manga, and winded up dropping off the map. I hate to see that, and I feel terrible when it happens.

KOSEI: It's a tough industry, eh? I'll do my best not to be just another guy who fades away and drops out. Say I leave today, start copying my favorite manga, and come up with that answer about what I'm trying to achieve. If I bring you a new sample after doing all that, will you teach me techniques I can put to use?

SAITO: Putting the techniques to effective use depends on you and what sort of series you're creating. But yes, I can tell you what you need to know, little by little, one step at a time.

KOSEI: That's good enough for me! I'll do it little by little! Until one day, I won't be a trend chaser, but a trendsetter!

SAITO: Glad to hear it! You should know, I've never once thought, "This is trendy in all the right ways, so let's make it into a series!" And I've never heard that sentiment expressed within editorial. What makes me happiest is identifying the seed of something great within a creator that we can then nurture together.

KOSEI: Sure, I get it!

SAITO: Keep in mind, figuring out what direction to take your work in doesn't mean that creating a one-shot of several dozen pages will suddenly be a walk in the park. It's fine to start out simple, with manga that's as short as even one or two panels. Doing a number of shorter works can easily lead you to ideas for longer stories and more involved characters, and along the way, your physical skills will also improve.

KOSEI: Then that's what I'll try! Um, can I ask another question though?

■ What are the fundamental steps on the road to getting serialized in *Jump*?

KOSEI: What does an author need to do to get serialized in *Jump*? I tried looking it up but didn't really find an answer anywhere.

SAITO: Hopeful authors will either bring in a sample to us, as you've done today, or they'll submit an entry either physically or digitally to any number of newcomer manga contests. Each contest has its own criteria, required page count, content theme, and judging process, so I would direct you to the *Weekly Shonen Jump* website, where you can read more about the different options.

KOSEI: If I win one of the contests hosted by *Jump* editorial, does that guarantee me a spot in the magazine?

SAITO: No. Generally speaking, after winning a contest, your next goal is getting a polished one-shot into either our sister magazine known as *Jump GIGA*, or the online publication Jump+. You'd work on the storyboards for that with an assigned editor in the hope of getting the green light from the editorial committee. Some authors may skip the contests altogether and come directly to us with storyboards good enough to win the committee's approval right off the bat. Assuming the one-shot in *Jump GIGA* or Jump+ is well received by readers, you would aim to get a one-shot into *Weekly Shonen Jump* proper. Assuming *that* one went over well, you'd start putting together a plan to wow the editorial committee with a full-blown series. Get the stamp of approval at that stage, and then, at last, you're serialized in *Jump*. Step-by-step, the process is, 1) bring in a sample or enter a contest, 2) get a one-shot in a sister magazine, 3) get a one-shot in *Jump*, and 4) get serialized in *Jump*.

KOSEI: So nobody skips all the steps and gets serialized right away, I guess...

SAITO: What I've just outlined is the standard route. In special cases, an author might blow the committee away and jump straight to their big debut. Others might debut in Jump+ before getting serialized in *Shonen Jump*.

KOSEI: Oh yeah? Are there any other routes you haven't mentioned?

■ Can I get published in *Jump* using a series that I've already put up on the internet?

SAITO: There are some authors who made their debuts in other magazines first, like *We Never Learn*'s Taishi Tsutsui Sensei. He happened to be an acquaintance of mine, and after one thing led to another, we started going over the storyboards that would eventually lead to his serialization in *Jump*. He's just one example like that. Other authors could have nothing to do with *Jump* at first, but when they start uploading manga they're working on to Twitter or the image board pixiv, I or another editor might notice it and reach out to them. From there, we can begin the process toward helping them make their official serialized debut in a web magazine.

KOSEI: But not a debut in the actual *Weekly Shonen Jump*?

SAITO: That hasn't happened so far. But we've certainly made contact with authors who post manga on social media, and we're imagining that going forward, that will become a more and more common route for authors to make their debuts.

KOSEI: Hmm. I was hoping for an easier path, but you're kinda telling me there isn't one...

SAITO: Ha ha! Even athletes and pop stars have to train and lay the groundwork before their careers can take off. Or what about all the studying and standardized tests that lawyers and doctors have to deal with? You'll be better off once you accept that becoming a professional manga author involves that same sort of diligence and patience. Still, you will have rare cases like Ryo Nakama Sensei, whose series *Isobe Isobee Monogatari: Ukiyo wa Tsurai yo* secured full-blown serialization, just six months after its debut. I believe the fastest path to serialization and one that will prepare you for the real struggles once you've made it, is not to desperately search for some elusive shortcut, but rather to assume there is no shortcut, and to approach the work head-on, with earnestness. Ask yourself, "**Do I want to create manga**?" and "**Do I want to be a professional manga author**?" Without the former as a goal, achieving the latter is going to be painfully difficult. Remember that, if nothing else.

KOSEI: Yeah, I get what you're saying. But I definitely wanna get an awesome manga published in *Jump* someday, so the first thing I will do is that copying practice you talked about! Once that gives me an idea of what I really wanna draw, I'll get back in touch with you about bringing in my next sample!

CHAPTER 1 KEY POINTS

- At the core of manga is the desire to create something, and then the ability to do so. Start off by thinking about what it is you want to draw and where your likes and interests lie.

- If you try to make manga without first knowing what you want to draw, and instead rely on rule books about inventing characters or stories or even chase trends that you're not personally fond of, you will inevitably find heartache and struggle.

TRY IT OUT

▷ Physically reproduce your favorite manga, by hand, whether it be a hit series, a one-shot, or even a single chapter. This is bound to lead to major discoveries. You can make your copy either by drawing it freehand or by tracing. Pencil or ballpoint pen is fine, but if you happen to have manga pens and draft paper or some sort of digital drawing device, using those tools of the trade at this stage can be great practice for later.

▷ Fill an entire notebook with short manga. They can be as short as a couple pages, or even just a single panel or two.

RUDIMENTARY MANGA KNOWLEDGE

Answers to some of the most frequent questions

from newcomers who bring us their samples!

What's a storyboard?

The storyboard is the most bare-bones stage of your draft, and is made long before the finished product. It shows your page and panel layout and indicates the story you want to tell. Authors often do this in notebooks, on printer paper, or digitally on a tablet.

Since it's so difficult to revise plot flow and page layout once your work is on draft paper, think of the storyboard as the essential blueprint for your manga. In chapter 2, we've included examples of storyboards from pro authors!

What's the title page?

Think of this as the cover for an individual chapter of manga. For an example, see the first page of the *One Piece* completed draft sample at the end of this at the end of this book, on page 183.

Can I handwrite my dialogue?

With a standard or mechanical pencil? Sure, why not? When your manga is being prepared for a magazine or online publication, the editor or print shop will pick out appropriate fonts for you.

What's an underdrawing? And what's inking?

After the storyboards comes the underdrawing, which is a slightly less rough draft done on draft-sized paper. Once that's done, you move on to inking (the actual lines present in the final product). Different authors put different amounts of detail into their underdrawings; some might fill in every last detail at that stage, while others will keep it loose and rough.

Many authors will photocopy their storyboards and blow them up to draft size before using a light box to trace and create the underdrawing.

I don't know the difference between the left and right pages.

Unless the editor tells you otherwise, Japanese manga always starts on the left page, while comics in the left-to-right reading order start on the right page. In terms of page numbers, that places a right-to-left page 1 on the left, page 2 on the right, page 3 on the left, and so on. "Left hand odd, right hand even" is probably the easiest way to remember!

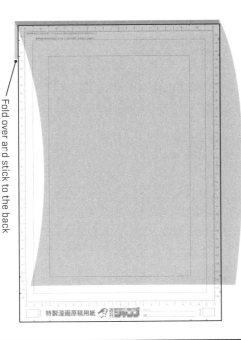

Fold over and stick to the back

How do I go about writing my dialogue on top of the drawings?

Use that very thin paper known as tracing paper.

① Stick the tracing paper on top of your manga page, fold the top edge over, and tape it to the back.

② Handwrite your dialogue on the tracing paper in all the appropriate spots.

③ Cut out the dialogue and paste it to your draft. Cut pieces that are bigger than needed, because tiny fragments of tracing paper could easily fall off and get lost.

How thick should the panel borders be? How wide should the gutters between panels be?

There's no strict standard, but panel borders range from 0.3 to 1 mm thick. The vertical gap between panels should be 2 to 4 mm, while the horizontal gap is between 5 and 10 mm. When *Shonen Jump* is blown up 1.2 times, that gives you B4 draft paper size, more or less, so feel free to refer to your favorite manga when preparing your draft.

What do I do about the title logo for my series?

When it's time to publish (either in a magazine or on the web), the editor will usually request a logo from a designer. Of course, you're free to do that part of the job yourself too!

Can I change the type of draft paper I'm using partway through, and if I mess up a panel, can I cut it out and patch in a new one?

Unshapely, unsightly draft pages? Not a problem at all. The content is what really matters. Even pros submit ugly stuff sometimes.

I don't understand how to use draft paper properly.

It's hard to know where to start with this type of paper, but whether working analog or digitally, it's always the same. Standardized draft paper shows lines for the "safety" (270 mm wide by 180 mm tall), the "trim line" (310 mm by 220 mm), and the outer edge of the "bleed." Digital draft paper also has these three clearly defined borders.

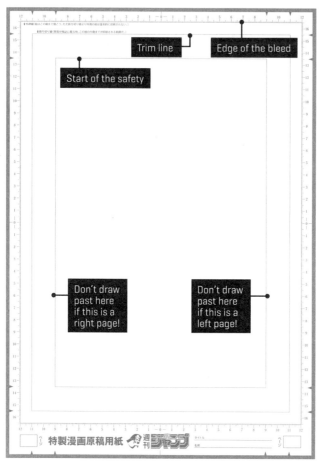

Trim line

Edge of the bleed

Start of the safety

Don't draw
past here
if this is a
right page!

Don't draw
past here
if this is a
left page!

☆ **Using draft paper the right way differs depending on whether it's the left or right page.**

When you open a magazine, the little valley between the pages in the center is called the "gutter." Anything on the page that extends beyond the start of the safety can be swallowed up in the gutter, so it's best not to have any dialogue or important parts of your art past that line. For a right-hand page, you want to stop drawing before the left-hand safety, and vice versa.

☆ **For particularly bold and impactful scenes, you may have the art extend into the safety as far as the trim line.**

When doing so, note the following points:

① Any art beyond the trim line will generally not be printed.

② However, when the magazine or volume is trimmed to size at the print shop, some variation may occur, so a best practice is to continue the art 5 mm beyond the trim line.

③ Similarly, the print shop could chop your page a few millimeters *before* the trim line, so character faces, dialogue, and handwritten text should be kept out of the safety.

NUMBER ONE FREQUENTLY ASKED QUESTION:
How do I use double-page spread paper?

A double-page spread is a situation where the images on the left and right sides join in the middle, contiguously. You can see an example of this on the fourth and fifth pages of the *One Piece* draft sample in this book.

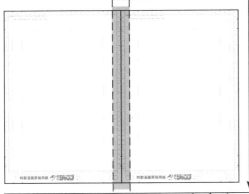

Literally cut and paste along the trim line!

THE METHOD:

① Trim your two pages at their respective inner trim lines, and tape them together from behind. We recommend masking tape, which tends to be sturdy enough.

② Like ordinary pages, your double-page spread will be printed up to the trim line, going all around.

③ The very center of the double-page spread will be swallowed up in the middle of the magazine or book, so keep any important art or dialogue away from that center line.

☆ **See chapter 5 for an explanation on doing double-page spreads for a digital draft!**

CHAPTER 2

LET'S CREATE A TWO-PAGE MANGA

After his first visit to the office, Kosei went home and started practicing with the goal of envisioning the manga he wants to create. Now he's back and ready to present Saito with a new sample.

Plus, we've asked four pro manga authors to create two-page manga based on the same prompts. Comparing the results and seeing how they approached the challenge in their own unique ways just goes to show that there's no single "correct" way to make manga.

■ How do I decide page layouts?

KOSEI: Hi, remember me? I'm back with my second sample!

SAITO: Thanks for dropping by again. Hmm, hang on—that envelope looks pretty slim.

KOSEI: Yeah, well... After last time, I went home and started copying some manga, just like you said. Doing that a bunch got me really hyped, so I dropped everything and started working on an original fifty-page manga. The problem was, the story just wasn't holding together, and no matter how much I drew, it didn't feel like I was making real progress... Still, I knew I had to show you something, so I came here today with two totally finished pages. Ones I really put my heart into.

SAITO: Very well—this is what I'll critique today. It may only be two pages, but I'm still impressed at the level of polish, with inking and everything! You've also made sure to draw the faces nice and large. That's good.

KOSEI: Ah... It doesn't just look like I'm using close-ups to hide everything else?

SAITO: Not at all. **Drawing faces is terribly important in manga**. What's the first thing that makes readers fall in love with a character? The faces and expressions, of course. A face can communicate so much raw information and emotion—when I see a newcomer drawing close-ups of faces in their one-shot, that automatically earns a point of praise.

KOSEI: I think I'm learning a little!

SAITO: That said...you could have used some more empty space.

KOSEI: What do you mean?

SAITO: There's almost too much information crammed in here. You've got every panel packed with characters and dialogue.

KOSEI: Sure, I wanted to include every idea I thought of, and I only had two pages to do it.

SAITO: Having a wealth of ideas is great, but those ideas backfire when they make your comic less readable. Readers will have an easier time processing if you zoom the camera out, so to speak, and reduce the amount of dialogue to create more empty space.

KOSEI: So my manga isn't any good?

SAITO: I'm not discrediting the clear effort that went into this, nor any of the ideas within. My point is that **you want to have visual variety between panels**.

KOSEI: Variety? How so?

SAITO: From the start, **figure out your priorities for each page and decide which panel is the most important**. Kentaro Yabuki Sensei had the right idea when he said, "**Think of your two opposing pages—left and right—as a single, cohesive piece of art**." His point was that authors should look at each pair of pages and decide how to arrange the art and word balloons with harmony, such that they create a pleasing reading experience. In your two-page manga here, you've approached each individual panel as its own distinct drawing, so despite your best efforts, it's hard to retain the information while reading.

KOSEI: Now that you mention it, when I take a step back and look at it objectively... Yeah, this is hard to read.

SAITO: For any given pair of pages, you should have **the key, standout panel take up about one-quarter of the space**. Then, create some contrast and variety by purposely making all the other panels smaller.

KOSEI: That's definitely easier said than done. Can you show me what you mean, please?

REGARDING PAGE LAYOUT:

① Pick the standout panel (the star attraction of the page or spread) and make it noticeably bigger than all other panels.

② Having *some* panels full of close-ups and dialogue is fine, but be sure to include panels that also show the characters' full bodies.

NOW, FOCUS ON APPLYING THOSE PRINCIPLES. BEYOND THAT, DRAW WHAT YOU WANT TO AND BREAK UP THE PAGES HOWEVER YOU'D LIKE! YOU'RE SURE TO IMPROVE WITH PRACTICE!!

*There are times when those two rules can be ignored. Every rule has its exception! That's just how manga rolls!

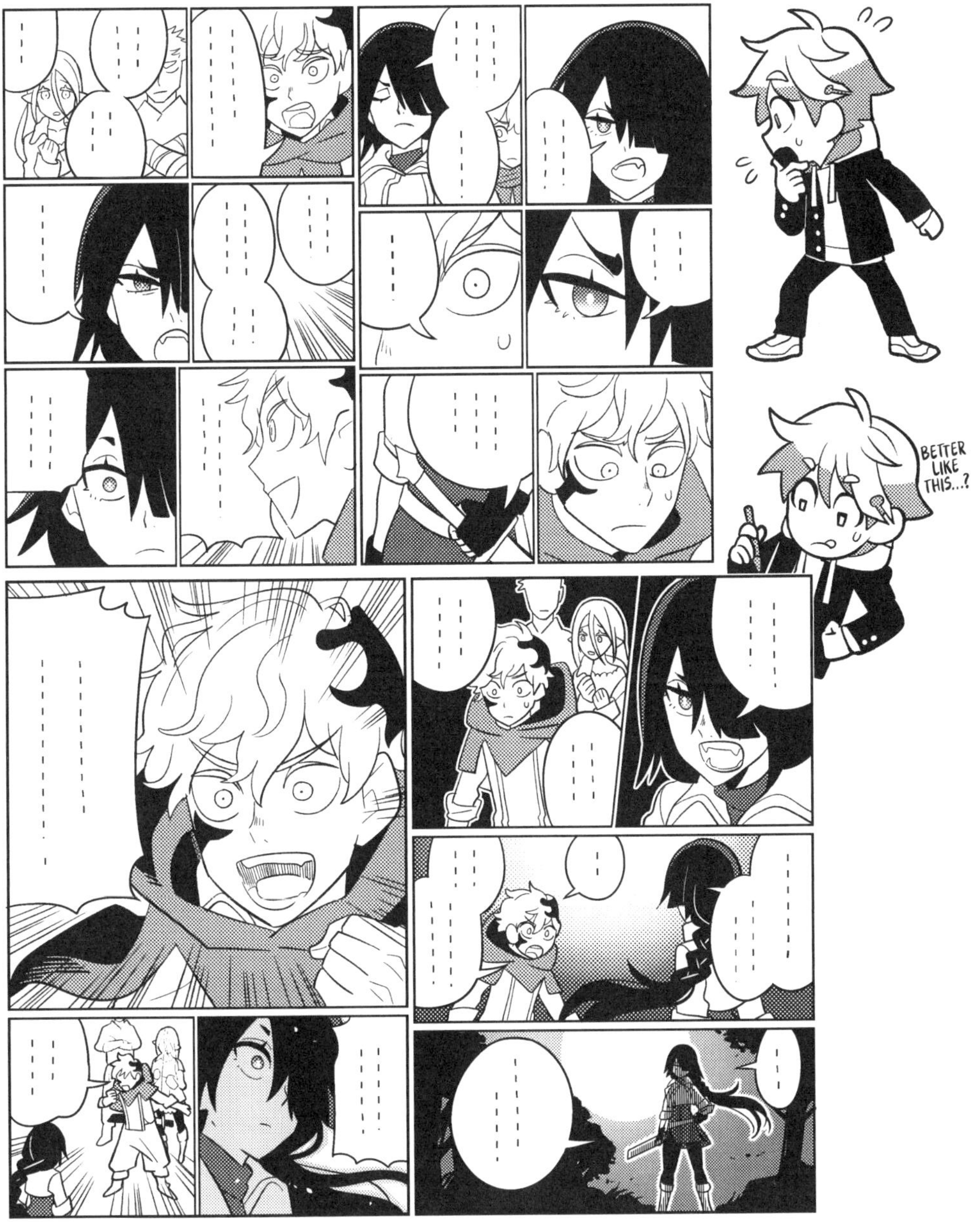
BETTER LIKE THIS...?

■ Examine these storyboards and learn how the authors used different layouts for the same prompts.

SAITO: You'll get the hang of these things after drawing enough two-page manga. It's great practice for learning to quickly get to the point in your stories, as well as giving you a sense for good page layout—the perfect bridge between the copying exercise and actually creating storyboards for a one-shot. **Starting with two pages is much more manageable than suddenly trying to produce dozens**, right? We recently asked a number of pro manga authors to produce two-page manga given the same two prompts. Care to take a look? Now that you've created a two-page manga, you can even compare your results to theirs. That can tell you something about the unique way you tend to portray things, and it can make you more aware where your work might fall short.

KOSEI: Wow, you mean it? Yeah, I'd love to check those out!

SAITO: Another point—when drawing all by your lonesome, it's hard to get a sense of **how much information can and should be included in any given set of two pages**. That's one reason we asked these four *Jump* authors to do these two-page stories for us.

KOSEI: I've always dreamed of creating some long, epic tale, so it never occurred to me to write short, snappy stories like this. This is probably a better way to practice than trying to craft the next epic tale, huh?

SAITO: Nobody's suggesting that you should specialize in these short sprints, but even long-distance runners have the stamina for shorter bursts. Crafting a concise story in manga form is a skill of its own, but doing many of **these shorter-form works will help you** develop the stamina needed to tackle proper one-shots and long series. Just like with the copying exercise, practice makes perfect!

KOSEI: Sure, I'll do what I can!

SAITO: After reading through these examples by the pros, don't just go, "Wow, I like these!," and let it end there. I want you to reflect on what you observe and then start drawing more of your own, on your own. Still, keep in mind that when it comes to implementing a setup and a punch line in such a short span, these authors are, well, professionals. Your goal at first should be to create a **two-page story that's readable**.

PROMPT ①

Two high school boys on their way home come across a purse snatcher and put a stop to the crime (how they do so is up to you).

PROMPT ②

An employee (of any gender) who's just been fired from their job is moping in a public park. A concerned child gives them a stag beetle to cheer them up, which kind of works.

バイク、体
浮き上がる
Motorcycle and thief's
body lift up into the air

Bag goes flying (とぶ バッグ)

A solid, open-hand slap
強烈な張り手

Thief
犯人

Ⓐ

Bag バッグ

Motorcycle バイク

Thief 犯人

Huhh?

(A)'s hand

Ⓐ

Ⓐ

Thief 犯人

Ⓐ の手

Thief 犯人

Ⓑ

The friend
友人好

Main girl
ヒロイン

*School building

(時計 下校時刻)
(Clock indicates going-home time)

*Route to and from school

キャーひったくり

Eek! He snatched my bag!

ヒロイン女子の友だち
Main girl's friend

ヒロイン女子
Main girl

Random person (helping)
モブ (助ける3)

どけどけどけえ!!

The victim (overcome with grief)
被害者 (悲しみ 困る)

The friend
友人女子

(モブ)
Random person

ヒロイン女子
Main girl

Outta my damn way!!

The bag he snatched
ひったくったバッグ

Thief
ひったくり犯

Thief
(Make him look as dastardly as possible)
ひったくり犯
(で もう見限り)
(車を引に)

ハヤク
猛スピード
Roaring, high-speed motorcycle

(Whipping out phone, or whatever) (スマホ 出手など)

High school boys 男子高生
Ⓐ
Ⓑ

気がく
They notice

Sumo type (big/brawny)
*Keep them obscured in this panel (just silhouettes)

Slim, handsome type

See page 52 for commentary!

47

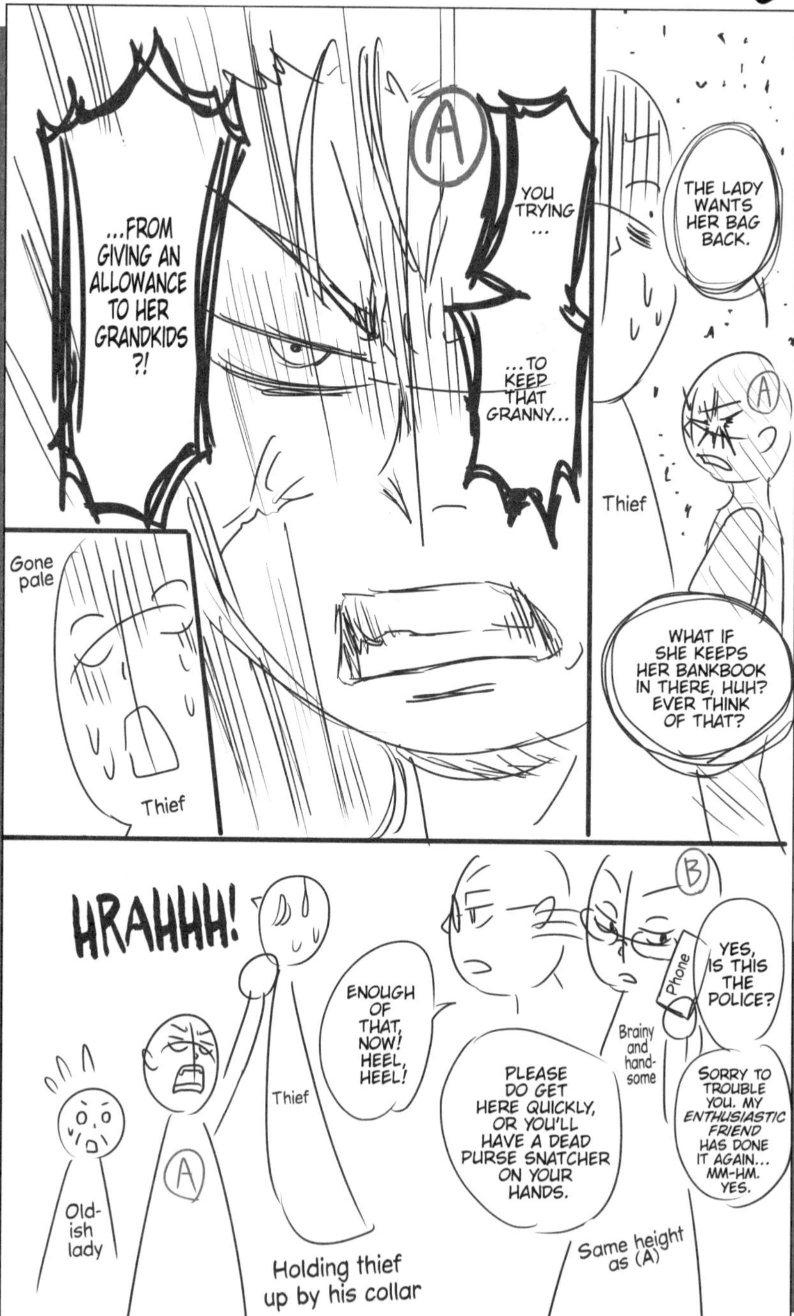
THE LADY WANTS HER BAG BACK.
Thief
A
WHAT IF SHE KEEPS HER BANKBOOK IN THERE, HUH? EVER THINK OF THAT?
A
YOU TRYING...
...TO KEEP THAT GRANNY...
...FROM GIVING AN ALLOWANCE TO HER GRANDKIDS?!
Gone pale
Thief
B
YES, IS THIS THE POLICE?
Phone
SORRY TO TROUBLE YOU. MY ENTHUSIASTIC FRIEND HAS DONE IT AGAIN... MM-HM. YES.
Brainy and hand-some
Same height as (A)
PLEASE DO GET HERE QUICKLY, OR YOU'LL HAVE A DEAD PURSE SNATCHER ON YOUR HANDS.
ENOUGH OF THAT, NOW! HEEL, HEEL!
HRAHHH!
Thief
Holding thief up by his collar
A
Old-ish lady

See page 65 for commentary!

TAISHI TSUTSUI

8

PROMPT ①

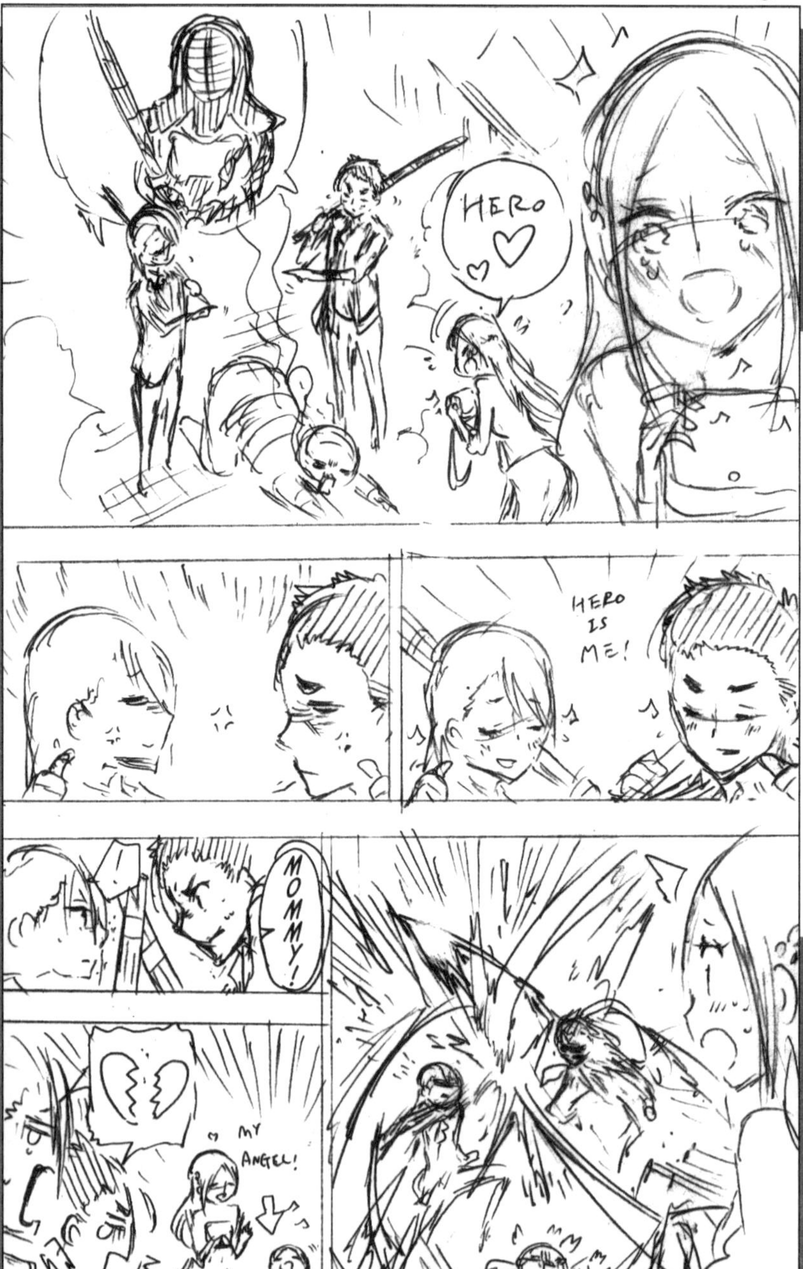
HERO
HERO IS ME!
MOMMY!
MY ANGEL!

See page 54 for commentary!

PROMPT 1

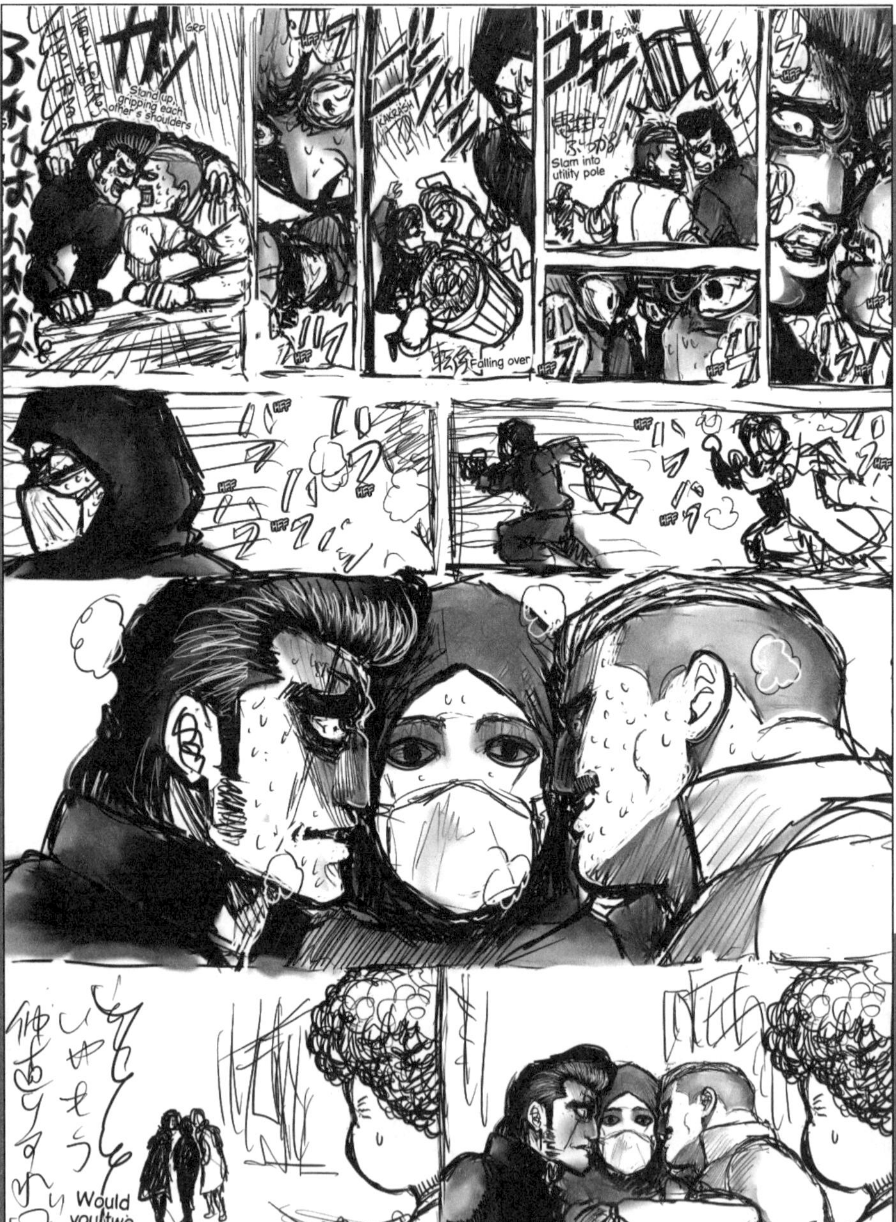
HFF
BONK
Slam into utility pole
HFF
Falling over
GRP
Stand up, gripping each other's shoulders
HFF
HFF
HFF
Would you two kiss and make up already?!

See page 55 for commentary!

Kaiu Shirai Sensei's Commentary

With both prompts, my strategy was to pick one thing I really wanted to show while shaving away pretty much everything else. The assignment seemed to be a challenge to include as much stuff as possible in just two pages. Still, I set out to showcase what needed to be shown with as *little* information as possible, while keeping the layouts from feeling too empty (due to lack of information).

STORYBOARD ①

What I wanted to show was some cool bits from an artistic perspective (making the reader eager to get to the next page) and then a drawing that gets the reader to stop and stare. As a writer, my storyboard is really more of a road map that would heavily rely on the hypothetical series artist to flesh out the art.

First, I needed a single moment with a thrilling counterattack against the low-down, no-good bag snatcher. I had a number of thoughts, but then my head conjured the image of someone using pure force to stop the motorcycle and make it flip into the air. The art for this moment had to be flashy and interesting, but it also had to serve as a sudden shock, so I stuck it at the top of the left page, and made it as large as possible.

Then, to lend that most important moment the maximum impact, I increased the density of the panels on the right-hand page (and instead of having the very first panel rise up to the trim line, I brought it back down to the start of the safety). I wanted the surprise to come not only from the attack on the thief, but from the appearance of the boys in and of itself, so I barely showed the boys at all on the first page, opting to focus instead on the eyewitnesses—the girl and her friend. It was also essential to communicate just how nasty and despicable this thief was on the right-hand page. All of this combines to make the big action moment even more awesome and rewarding. The top panel on the left is also made more exciting in comparison by making the last panel on the right especially small.

I decided to make the boy who fights back a sumo wrestler. Typically, a standard muscly boy would be good enough, but I thought that putting a sumo boy in the school uniform could grab the reader's attention. If this were a thirty- to forty-page one-shot, it would cut down on a bunch of exposition; this awesome scene and the resulting characterization would allow me to devote more panel time to other stuff.

If they'd let me use four pages total for this little story, I would've devoted the entire second page to that one moment of impact, followed by a bunch of panels where the thief and his motorcycle fly into the air before crashing down, and finally, I would've ended with the sumo boy striking a powerful pose. But with only two pages available, I had to pare things down.

Rather than worry about working in a grand finale, telling a complete story, or including everything possible, I approached this task with the goal of creating the necessary excitement to justify that one bit of art I wanted to include. To that end, I tossed away intrusive thoughts like "don't need this" or "can't do this" (hoping to win more points, rather than just avoid losing points, if you get what I mean).

Taishi Tsutsui Sensei's Commentary

WHAT I KEPT IN MIND WHILE DRAWING

I kept dialogue to the absolute minimum for both prompts, opting instead to communicate the stories as clearly as possible through the art alone.

STORYBOARD ①

I wanted the premise of "high school boys catch a purse snatcher" to come across very clearly from a visual standpoint, so I made the boys rivals in the kendo club. With only two pages to work with, I had to be stingy with exposition, which meant giving readers the whole setup in the very first panel. You've got two high school boys with *shinai* sword bags walking past the school building, which tells you they're on their way home. They're glancing to their right, which guides the reader's line of sight to the left, where the reader will spot, in order, the victim, the stolen bag, and the thief.

The next thing I focused on was giving the characters motivation. You've got this gorgeous woman occupying the right side of the page, and then immediately, the boys' reaction. This communicates to the reader very clearly that the boys are motivated to earn the pretty woman's affection. It gives extra importance to their quest. But this little story would fall flat if they caught the thief and that was that. So instead, the final punch line ties back to their initial motivation.

Two pages don't provide enough room for an extended action sequence, so the only taste of action comes at the bottom of the first page. By having the conclusion of the action scene in the very next panel, I've only used two panels total, while giving the reader enough context to fill in the gap with their imagination.

That same panel (the first on page 2) shows both the joyful woman with her bag and an overhead view of the whole scene, which tells you everything you need to know about how the fight ended. The boys point at each other and their word balloon shows a fully equipped kendo practitioner, which is them telling the woman that they're both in the kendo club. Then each calls himself a hero, as if to suggest, "My pal here is just your average member of the kendo club, but yes, I'm a hero." Each boy tries to take all the credit and win the woman's heart, which provides instant characterization. When they start sparring with each other, the reader realizes that the boys are truly rivals on roughly equal footing.

The aforementioned motivation is brought back into play when the appearance of the woman's daughter tells the boys and the reader that the woman probably isn't on the prowl for a boyfriend. Instant heartbreak—that's our punch line.

Hideaki Sorachi Sensei's Commentary

For the first prompt, the purse snatcher, I made use of the double-hero setup and had them fighting each other. At first, though, I had tons of dialogue and action overwhelming the pages (with a setup and punch line in every panel), which was total info overload. So I removed the dialogue, prioritized telling the story with the art, and chopped up the panels.

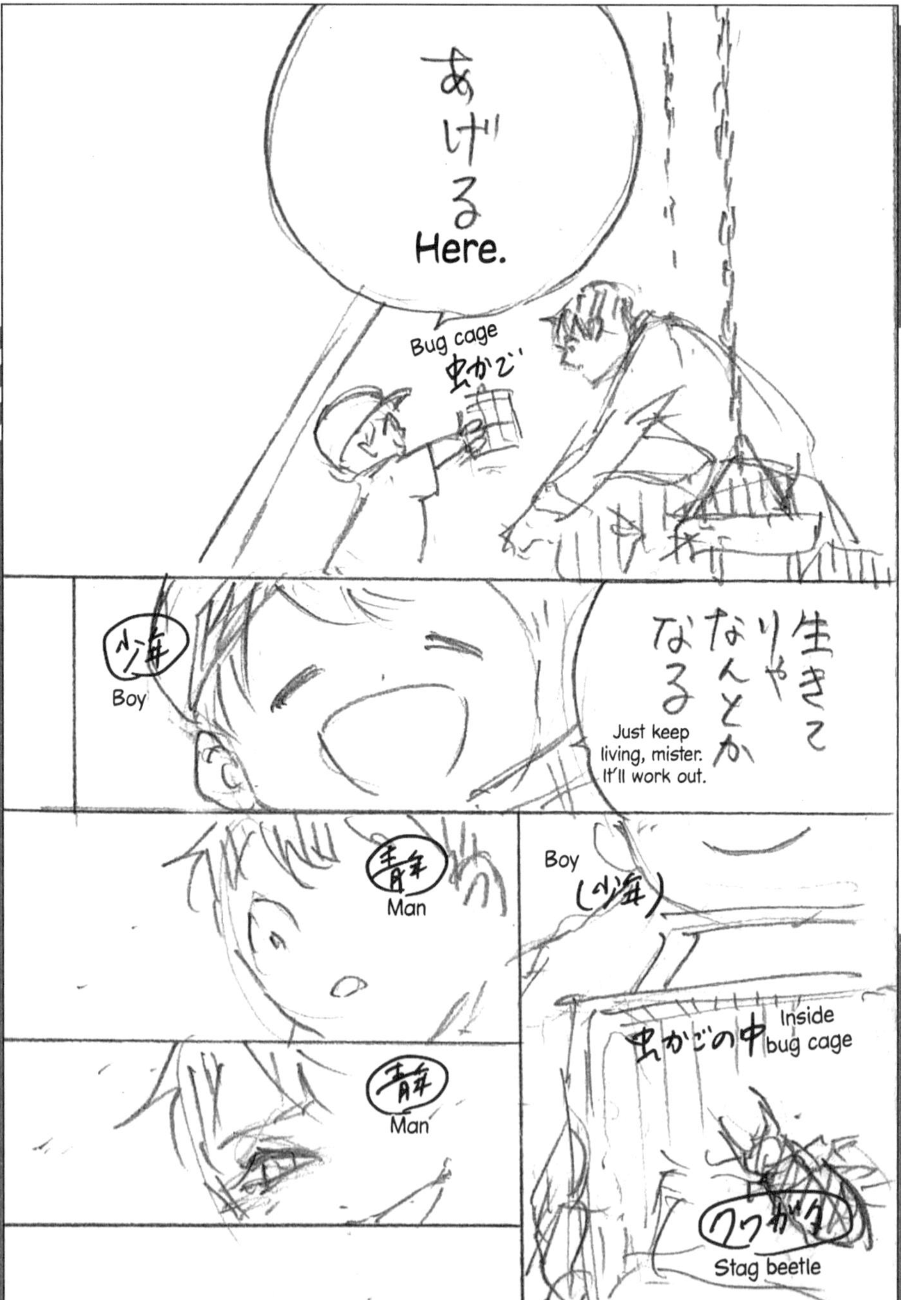
あげる
Here.
Bug cage
虫かご
生きてりゃなんとかなる
Just keep living, mister. It'll work out.
少年
Boy
Boy
(少年)
虫かごの中
Inside bug cage
クワガタ
Stag beetle
青年
Man
青年
Man

See page 64 for commentary!

YUTO TSUKUDA

2

Stag beetle

GEEZ, I FEEL BAD FOR YOU, MISTER!

LIKE CLEANUP TIME AND GETTING THE NEWSPAPER!

EVEN I GOT JOBS TO DO!

GLOOM

YEAH... NOT GONNA LIE. IT SUCKS.

SKWRM SKWRM

Girl's hand

IF YOU NEED WORK TO DO, YOU CAN TAKE CARE OF MR. BEETLE!

BUT YOU BETTER DO A GOOD JOB, OKAY?

Opening lid of bug cage

OH, I KNOW...

YOWCH!

I'LL... DO MY BEST, I GUESS...

Somehow glad to have a "job" to do

Took the beetle

BYE-BYE, MISTER!

See page 65 for commentary!

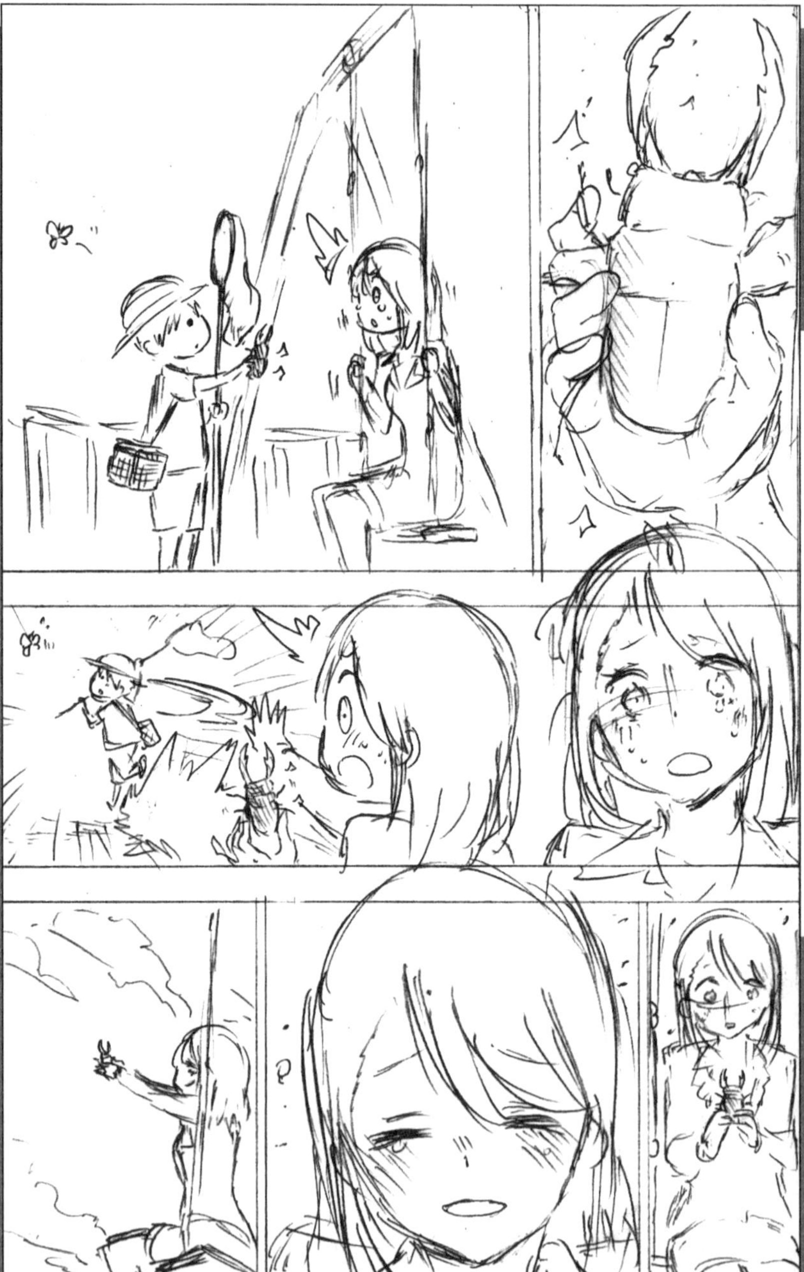

See page 65 for commentary!

PROMPT ②

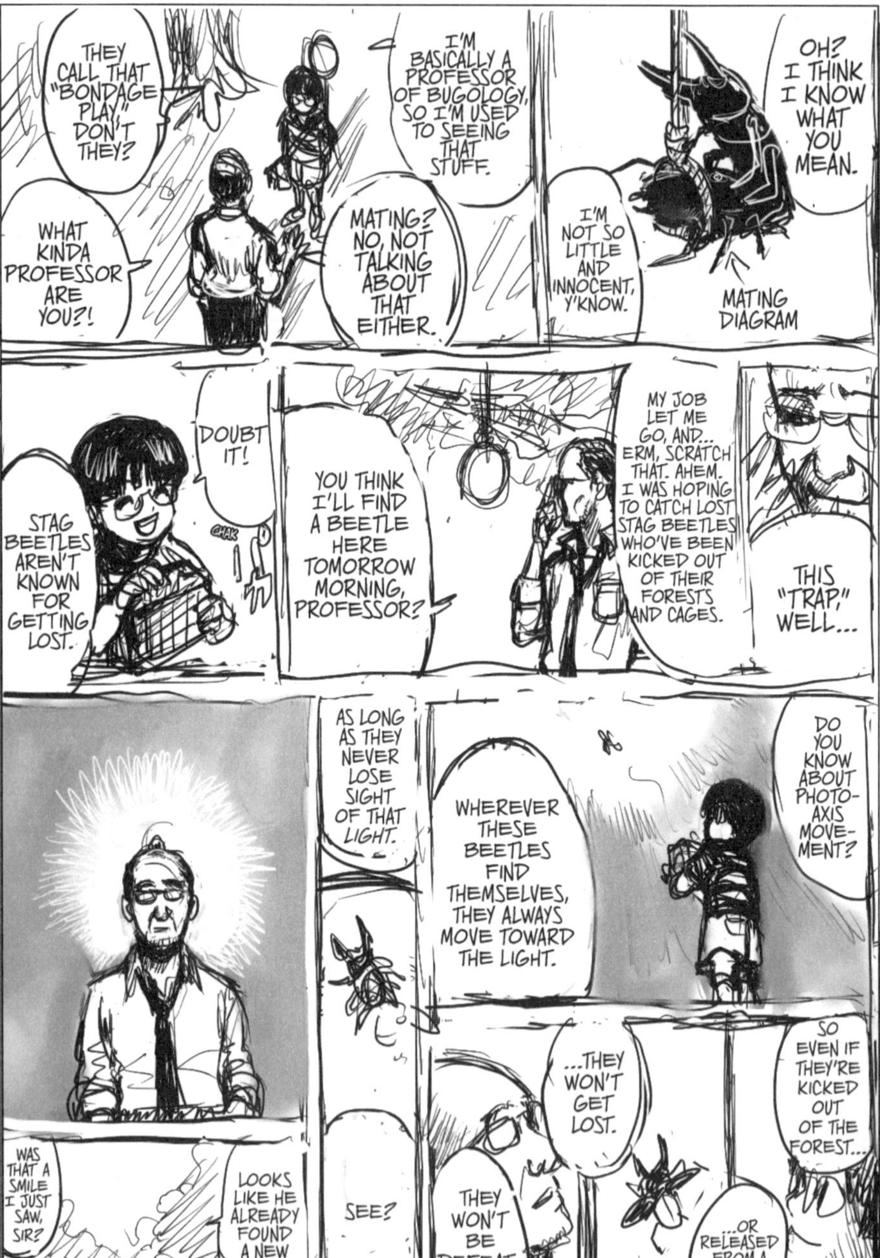
OH? I THINK I KNOW WHAT YOU MEAN.
MATING DIAGRAM
I'M NOT SO LITTLE AND INNOCENT, Y'KNOW.
I'M BASICALLY A PROFESSOR OF BUGOLOGY, SO I'M USED TO SEEING THAT STUFF.
MATING? NO, NOT TALKING ABOUT THAT EITHER.
THEY CALL THAT "BONDAGE PLAY," DON'T THEY?
WHAT KINDA PROFESSOR ARE YOU?!
THIS "TRAP," WELL...
MY JOB LET ME GO, AND... ERM, SCRATCH THAT. AHEM. I WAS HOPING TO CATCH LOST STAG BEETLES WHO'VE BEEN KICKED OUT OF THEIR FORESTS AND CAGES.
YOU THINK I'LL FIND A BEETLE HERE TOMORROW MORNING, PROFESSOR?
DOUBT IT!
CHAK
STAG BEETLES AREN'T KNOWN FOR GETTING LOST.
DO YOU KNOW ABOUT PHOTO-AXIS MOVEMENT?
WHEREVER THESE BEETLES FIND THEMSELVES, THEY ALWAYS MOVE TOWARD THE LIGHT.
AS LONG AS THEY NEVER LOSE SIGHT OF THAT LIGHT.
SO EVEN IF THEY'RE KICKED OUT OF THE FOREST...
...OR RELEASED FROM A BUG CAGE...
...THEY WON'T GET LOST.
THEY WON'T BE DEFEATED.
SEE?
LOOKS LIKE HE ALREADY FOUND A NEW HOME. PFFT!
WAS THAT A SMILE I JUST SAW, SIR?

See page 69 for commentary!

Kaiu Shirai Sensei's Commentary

STORYBOARD ②

Most likely, the by-the-book approach would be to tell this story from the perspective of the adult who's just lost their job. Maybe that's what they wanted us to do? But when I tried it that way, what I came up with fell flat and didn't feel like my work at all, so I switched to the boy's perspective.

More than just the gift of the stag beetle, it's the boy's pure, innocent warmth that manages to cheer up the man. That's how I interpreted the prompt anyway, so what I wanted to portray most was the boy's kindness, which cheers up the guy who's been sacked. That's why I positioned the panel where the boy says, "Here," as the most important one.

Cutting down on dialogue and telling the story through pauses and silence felt like a good way to make the "Here" stand out even more, so I ended up shaving away all but the "Here" and that one other line (having the man's termination implied by the paper in the briefcase eliminated the need for explaining it).

The second panel of the story communicates the setting (the park), and the size of the panel also suggests the severity of the man's gloominess. That said, I positioned it in such a way so as not to upstage the all-important "Here" panel. Beyond that, I adjusted each panel's size according to the importance of the information within.

In the event that the man's expression in the final panel couldn't properly communicate his thoughts ("Oh, how happy this has made me!"), I might have added another panel at the very end with him saying "Yeah!" or "Thanks!" However, I had already decided to use minimal dialogue. Just know that this version would be perfect if I could ask *The Promised Neverland*'s Posuka Demizu Sensei to do the art (which would result in the ideal expression for the man in that final panel). I hope that's good enough.

Yuto Tsukuda Sensei's Commentary

My focus for each of these was on how these characters necessarily *had* to be. For the first one, it was, "A guy who wouldn't hesitate even a little to stop a bag snatcher," and the second was, "Exactly the kind of kid who would give a stranger a beetle." The joke about the *hitoban* flying-head monster was something I had the urge to sketch out. Kids often know the weirdest trivia, right? And I added the bit about the reference book to flesh out the scene and make the random trivia more convincing. Finally, I tried to match each word balloon to the character and exact context so that even in panels where the people aren't shown, the reader has zero doubt about who's saying what.

Taishi Tsutsui Sensei's Commentary

STORYBOARD ②

The scene is set with a wide shot of the park, showing someone swinging rather gloomily. The swinger's identity is immediately revealed as the woman on the right side of the page, and the reader gets the impression that she is the main character. The prompt didn't specify gender, but I went with a woman because that's probably what readers expect from me. Just like with the first prompt, I didn't have a ton of space to tell this story, so I cut down the little flashback to the bare necessities.

FLASHBACK, PANEL 1

Close-up of the woman to start the flashback ➡ Coffee spills on the photocopier ➡ Smoke rises from the busted machine ➡ Her boss is mad ➡ The woman bows over and over as she apologizes.

FLASHBACK, PANEL 2

The boss tells the woman she's fired ➡ She expresses great shock.

In just two panels, the reader learns that the woman messed up at work and was fired for it.

We exit the flashback and return to the park (and the present timeline) via the trail of thought bubbles. The woman looks quite down in the dumps, but the reader gets a glimpse of the bug-catching child running around behind her, which is foreshadowing.

The final panel of page 1 suggests that something off panel is approaching the woman. Then, page 2 begins with an extreme close-up of the stag beetle to catch the reader off guard with the unexpected, followed by a wider shot that clearly explains the situation. I gave the boy a particularly blank expression so that the reader would have to infer his thoughts and feelings based on his actions.

Immediately after giving the woman the beetle, the boy runs off to chase a butterfly. This characterizes him as someone who loves bugs above all else and *nevertheless* gave his prized catch to the woman to cheer her up. That transforms his choice into the ultimate act of kindness.

For the final panel, I switch to a low angle that shows the sky, suggesting that the woman's mood has improved, and deliberately ending on a positive note.

Hideaki Sorachi Sensei's Commentary

Even with only two pages, I tried to see how much dialogue I could cram into the second prompt to make it driven by the conversation. A lot of my habits from *Gin Tama*'s chapter 1 one-shot have stuck, so I tend to set ease of reading aside and instead make each chapter 1 as dense as humanly possible. "Readability" is a foreign concept to me. Sorry.

■ Things to Consider when Creating a Two-Page Manga

SAITO: Well, any thoughts? Hmm? Kosei? Snap out of it.

KOSEI: Whoa. Those were all just about...a *billion* times better than the so-so two-page manga I brought in today. I'm kinda nervous now. Who knew so much thought went into making manga?

SAITO: These are all professionals with big hits under their belts, so don't let it get you down. Think about how many hundreds or thousands of pages they've drawn. Still, even I wasn't expecting such a variety of manga based on those prompts.

KOSEI: They managed to cram so much characterization into just two pages that I couldn't help but grin. Shirai Sensei always manages to include a big explosive surprise. Then you've got Tsutsui Sensei, who uses expressions and gestures to create the cutest women. And Tsukuda Sensei packs those two pages with passion, gags, and that distinct sense of weary relief. It's so good, I practically got chills.

SAITO: Indeed. On the one hand, you have Shirai Sensei, who decided to give the second prompt room to breathe and build, which made the scant dialogue on page 2 all the more meaningful. On the other hand, Tsutsui Sensei's goal is clear—scrap almost all dialogue in favor of showcasing women. Tsukuda Sensei chose to use actions and dialogue to lend clear characterization to his characters, which makes his work very readable. As for Sorachi Sensei... He resides in a different plane of existence than the rest of us. Most authors wouldn't dare start that prompt with something as dark as a noose made for suicide. And he's given so much raw energy to the weird grown men in the first prompt, you almost get the feeling that he's passionate about making his work as distinct from everyone else's as possible.

KOSEI: I was cracking up so hard at that...

SAITO: When you and I first met, I advised against starting with the more technical knowledge and suggested that you'd be better off slowly figuring out what sort of things you'd like to create. After seeing the storyboards from these four authors, is it a little clearer why **a strong vision is so much more important than technical skill when starting out**?

KOSEI: I guess, but the pros have insane technical skills too.

SAITO: That may be true, but what these works should tell you is that those technical skills exist in service of creating what the authors have decided to create. Remember how Sorachi Sensei said he started all over and chopped up the pages into many small panels *because* he only had two pages to work with? That creates a clear contrast between the larger drawings and the small, cramped ones.

KOSEI: Right... When I sat down to make my two-page manga, I wanted to include all my ideas, but I panicked and froze up when I realized that the comic wouldn't have room to breathe. None of those pauses. Page layout is tricky...

SAITO: Notice how Tsutsui Sensei usually features women's smiles and full body shots. Meanwhile, Tsukuda Sensei's highlights in both prompts are the top panels of the left-hand pages. These authors decide what the star player of the two pages is going to be and then position everything else around that.

KOSEI: Shirai Sensei seems to like those pauses and silences, Tsukuda Sensei takes us on a roller coaster of wild ups and downs, Tsutsui Sensei wants to draw cute girls, and Sorachi Sensei is all about drawing older dudes.

SAITO: Strangely enough, it's not just Sorachi Sensei. A surprising number of authors love drawing older men.

KOSEI: I guess it's all about cutting down on everything that's not what you're trying to show, and giving the panels variety, like you mentioned!

SAITO: Which you could look at as tempo. It's a difficult concept to teach someone, since it ties back to personal taste. Each author has their own tempo that feels just right to them.

KOSEI: "Tempo" feels a little too tied to intuition for me to get a handle on, but what I do understand is how you gotta **decide what you wanna draw, and then how to add emphasis or pull back**.

SAITO: You get the feeling that Sorachi Sensei's goal was to creep out the reader by moving closer and closer to these rugged, glaring ne'er-do-wells, and then have them fighting and flailing around just so they'd be drenched in sweat by the end. He started with that vision and figured out just the right way to portray it in comic form. Similarly, you should start by adjusting your work's tempo and emphasis according to your specific goal. Over time, you'll naturally improve on the finer points of page and panel layouts.

KOSEI: Sounds good to me. I'll try copying each of these two-page storyboards from the pros... That could give me insight into the points they're trying to get across and how they play around with panel variety.

SAITO: Seeing the pros' work may have sent you spiraling at first, but as long as you walk away with a sense of what you're trying to achieve and what matters most, it's all worthwhile. There's no sense in comparing your own work to theirs and beating yourself up. The greater takeaway should be that when it comes to manga, four different authors will produce four very different results, even with the same prompt. You asked me about the "correct" way to make manga when we first met, but each author created something unique and delightful, right? **Given the infinite possibilities, don't stress about accidentally creating something too similar to something else.** Focus on the positives and keep drawing more of your own stuff. Once you've grown accustomed to the two-page manga format, challenge yourself to draw a longer one-shot, which we'll be happy to provide feedback on. All at your own pace, of course.

CHAPTER 2 KEY POINTS

- Panel layout comes down to drawing characters' faces and communicating information to the reader. Your manga is easier to read if you include panels where the "camera" pulls back to show some empty space and panels that show characters' full bodies.

- Knowing what you want to show and what you want to draw is the starting point for page layout. From there, focus on panel variety. Beyond that, the details are really up to you.

TRY IT OUT

▷ When creating a longer manga feels too overwhelming, go for a simple two-page story.

▷ Filling your two-page story with a proper setup and punch line will be challenging at first. Your goal, first and foremost, should be readability.

FREQUENTLY ASKED QUESTIONS FROM NEW AUTHORS

PART 1

Q 1 I'm trying to enter manga contests, but I can never tell the full story I want to in such a limited number of pages.

A A typical serialized manga chapter is anywhere from ten pages to around forty pages, while an introductory chapter sometimes runs longer. Any good author needs the skills to tell stories with chapters of that length, so that's something to focus on as you practice. In the meantime, if you're having a hard time conceptualizing your story, think of one of your favorite series and write out, in detail, how one of those chapters is structured. Take a look at the rising action, climax, falling action, resolution, etc. On which page do each of those plot milestones begin, and how long do they last?

You'll tend to find plot development landmarks at page 4, page 19, page 31, and page 45. With that in mind, start with the elements of the story you want to draw the most, calculate back from that point, and shave off as much as you can until you're left with the essentials. You'll find that observing and analyzing the ins and outs of other series is a great way to grow as an author.

Your "textbook" in all this is any manga you find interesting. Steal what you can!

CHAPTER 3

JUMP AUTHOR SURVEYS

"Comparing my own two-page manga to those examples from the pros? Ohh, man. I think that may have killed off any confidence I might've had. As if I could never enter the ring with them!" whimpered Kosei.

"Don't be so hard on yourself," said Saito. "Every *Jump* author went through a similar period of growing pains."

This would-be reassurance didn't seem to cheer up Kosei much. Saito decided to survey a number of big-name *Jump* authors on their practice habits when starting out, what they bear in mind when creating, and other relevant things. "This is sure to contain valuable nuggets of knowledge," he thought, before sending the authors' survey answers off to Kosei.

THE QUESTIONS

1. What knowledge would have benefited you when starting your manga career?

2. What did you do first after deciding to become a manga author (e.g., practicing, strategizing, etc.), and/or did you have an efficient way to practice?

3. What are you mindful of when revising your own storyboards (either when self-editing or taking advice from editorial)?

4. Is there any way you could have been better prepared before your serialization began?

5. What do you bear in mind when creating manga (e.g., personal themes and through lines)?

6. What's your approach to creating strong, memorable characters?

7. How should one practice creating those strong characters?

8. How many works/pages did you create leading up to your first real submission? How many works/pages from that first submission until your magazine debut?

9. What's your approach to creating manga that's readable?

10. How long does it take to create the storyboards for a single nineteen-page chapter of manga?

11. How long does it take you to finish the full draft for a single nineteen-page chapter of manga?

12. Beyond creating your storyboards, what do you do to come up with ideas and plot points for your work?

13. Is there anything you referenced when creating your one-shots?

GEGE AKUTAMI

(Jujutsu Kaisen)

What knowledge would have benefited you when starting your manga career?

I wish my managing editor had sat me down and said, "Make your word balloons bigger" and "Don't break up your word balloons so much."

What did you do first after deciding to become a manga author (e.g., practicing, strategizing, etc.)? And/or, did you have an efficient way to practice?

Get in the habit of finishing what you start. Work on your ability to explain, in words, what you find exciting or boring about a given series. I found myself unable to focus on the art, so I would just do lots of quick, sketchy figure drawings (croquis). When I do a properly lit and shaded sketch (dessin) nowadays, I regret that I didn't adopt that habit sooner. I also regret having created so many rough storyboards, but basically no finished drafts.

What are you mindful of when revising your own storyboards (either when self-editing or taking advice from editorial)?

Since my work is published in a magazine for children, I'm always sure to listen when an editor tells me, "This part is hard to understand."

I try to plan out my storyboards with a strong sense of overall balance, and there've been many times when adjusting them based on the advice of others felt like removing pieces from a Jenga tower, which led to collapse and failure. Changing minor details is fine, but generally, I'd rather put in the work and start over from scratch instead of fixing up a bunch of things in my storyboards.

Is there any way you could have been better prepared before your serialization began?

I wish I'd had more experience doing proper drafts.

What do you bear in mind when creating manga (e.g., personal themes and throughlines)?

I'm not trying to get people from my own generation to come away thinking I have good taste.

What's your approach to creating strong, memorable characters?

Their mere appearance should elicit big laughs. Emphasis through repetition. Some sort of jarring discrepancy between expectations and reality.

Continued...

How should one practice creating those strong characters?

It comes down to imagining how other people will feel about your characters. Which is hard.

How many works/pages did you create leading up to your first real submission? How many works/pages from that first submission until your magazine debut?

Around age twenty, I tried to get my first short work (that is, a completed draft) into a magazine called *Aoharu*. I called about bringing in my work, but they sort of blew me off in a noncommittal way, so I gave up.

After that, I got two different one-shots into a sister magazine, two more one-shots in *Weekly Shonen Jump*, a four-chapter serialization in the monthly magazine (that run would eventually become *Jujutsu Kaisen* volume 0), and then finally my serialization in *WSJ*.

Between my first one-shot in the sister magazine and my second one in the main magazine, I honed my skills working under Kano Sensei (*Kiss x Death*).

What's your approach to creating manga that's readable?

I let my art blast right past the safety and trim lines in order to guide the reader's eye. That said, I tend to sacrifice readability for what I find interesting, so don't treat me like some sort of role model.

How long does it take to create the storyboards for a single nineteen-page chapter of manga?

It depends on the chapter, but usually around half a day. The weird thing is, even when I've got the story all thought out and I'm not unsure of anything, it can take me twelve hours or more just to get started on the storyboards (which only end up taking six or seven hours to finish). If, like me, you're the type of person who spends three hours psyching yourself up for a thirty-minute task, you might be in trouble if you're ever serialized in a manga magazine.

How long does it take you to finish the full draft for a single nineteen-page chapter of manga?

About five days. My focus is absolute garbage.

Beyond creating your storyboards, what do you do to come up with ideas and plot points for your work?

I recommend reading short stories (prose). Some of my best ideas come to me when I'm imagining how I would flesh out a short story into something longer.

Is there anything you referenced when creating your one-shots?

Collections of shorts from Haruko Ichikawa Sensei and Tomoko Yamashita Sensei. With one-shots, I'm thinking it might be better to make everything revolve around the intimate human drama, rather than the setup and the world.

EIICHIRO ODA

[One Piece]

What knowledge would have benefited you when starting your manga career?

Knowing what storyboards actually are. I would start telling my stories using full-on underdrawings instead.

(This was the era before the internet existed.)

What did you do first after deciding to become a manga author (e.g., practicing, strategizing, etc.)? And/or, did you have an efficient way to practice?

Drawing things realistically. Drawing Disney cartoons frame by frame. Drawing fashion show models at the same speed they popped out onto the catwalk.

What are you mindful of when revising your own storyboards (either when self-editing or taking advice from editorial)?

Coming to grips with my editor saying, "Right, that turned out how I thought." I start thinking about what led them to expect what was coming. A lot of the time, there's no clear reason.

Is there any way you could have been better prepared before your serialization began?

All the thinking in the world can't fully prepare you, so I say just go for it,

and once you've made it, then start panicking. You'll figure it out. Human beings are amazing that way.

What do you bear in mind when creating manga (e.g., personal themes and throughlines)?

I want to show readers something *new*.

Continued...

What's your approach to creating strong, memorable characters?

Distinct visual traits.

How should one practice creating those strong characters?

Observe people in real life.

How many works/pages did you create leading up to your first real submission? How many works/pages from that first submission until your magazine debut?

I drew manga in notebooks in sixth grade. One of my manga was a finalist in a contest in my first year of high school. In my final year of high school, they published my Tezuka Award–winning work "Wanted." I couldn't give you concrete numbers, but I've drawn every day since the moment I could.

What's your approach to creating manga that's readable?

Good phraseology.

How long does it take to create the storyboards for a single nineteen-page chapter of manga?

I like to finish within three days. If it takes longer, I just have to finish the draft quicker.

How long does it take you to finish the full draft for a single nineteen-page chapter of manga?

Three days, ideally. I'd take all the time in the world, if I could.

Beyond creating your storyboards, what do you do to come up with ideas and plot points for your work?

I take copious notes on movies and anything else remotely inspiring in everyday life. It's too easy to forget stuff otherwise.

Is there anything you referenced when creating your one-shots?

Nothing at all. How naive I was. The internet now makes it so easy to look stuff up, and everything you need to know about art is basically sitting there, so I say make use of those resources.

TITE KUBO

(Bleach, Burn the Witch)

What knowledge would have benefited you when starting your manga career?

Knowing about pen nibs, ink, types of paper, how to add floating text—meaning text not enclosed in word balloons—to my draft. I didn't know about that last thing until my editor taught me. I started dabbling in digital recently too. Apps, brushes, tools... I didn't know a thing about any of it, so it all feels so fresh and exciting!

What did you do first after deciding to become a manga author (e.g., practicing, strategizing, etc.)? And/or, did you have an efficient way to practice?

I bought a book called something like *Primer to Manga Techniques* that explained all the different tools. The info in that book allowed me to create all my manga.

What are you mindful of when revising your own storyboards (either when self-editing or taking advice from editorial)?

In my early days, I firmly believed that taking advice from an editor meant I had somehow lost a battle. Like it would all turn out okay if, even when ignoring the advice, what I created was well received.

When you're not feeling confident about this, that, or the other thing, set a time limit for yourself, and if you can't think up a way to improve before the self-imposed deadline, then send it off in spite of your concerns.

Don't say, "It could've been so much better if only I had more time." The normal response to that is, "Well, obviously. Duh."

Is there any way you could have been better prepared before your serialization began?

Nope. The learning happens on the job once you're serialized.

What do you bear in mind when creating manga (e.g., personal themes and throughlines)?

Variety and balance.

Continued...

What's your approach to creating strong, memorable characters?

I have to like the character, or at least have the potential to like them eventually. When I hate a character, I can't draw them in an appealing way. It's fine to be picky, but strive to broaden the range of what you personally find appealing.

How should one practice creating those strong characters?

Do it over and over. I mean, that makes sense, right?

How many works/pages did you create leading up to your first real submission? How many works/pages from that first submission until your magazine debut?

My first contest entry was a single work of thirty-one pages. The second thing I did was also thirty-one pages, but the serialization committee told me to add four pages, so I bumped it up to thirty-five and got it into the magazine.

What's your approach to creating manga that's readable?

Stick to vertical and horizontal panels. My editor when I was starting out said, "You have too many diagonally oriented panels," which really stuck with me.

How long does it take to create the storyboards for a single nineteen-page chapter of manga?

Three days. But the first three pages alone can take an entire day. Then I'll reach page eleven on day two and finish it off on day three.

How long does it take you to finish the full draft for a single nineteen-page chapter of manga?

For a chapter of a serialized work, it takes me ten to twelve hours to get the art on the page. Then another twenty hours once the assistants enter the picture.

Beyond creating your storyboards, what do you do to come up with ideas and plot points for your work?

I have a notebook to jot down faces and designs I think of. Now I also have a phone app that lets me write down potential dialogue, thoughts, names, items, etc., all categorized in different folders. A lot of those ideas happen to be magic related, partly because I was working on *Burn the Witch*.

Is there anything you referenced when creating your one-shots?

For *Burn the Witch*, I watched the *Kingsman* movie. I remember thinking how, in spy fiction, there's something cool about some everyday scenery suddenly flipping around (sometimes literally) to reveal something out of the ordinary.

KOYOHARU GOTOUGE

(Demon Slayer: Kimetsu no Yaiba)

What knowledge would have benefited you when starting your manga career?

Knowing from where to where you're supposed to draw on the draft paper. And how many centimeters of blank space should be left in the middle of the two pages, for the gutter.

What did you do first after deciding to become a manga author (e.g., practicing, strategizing, etc.)? And/or, did you have an efficient way to practice?

I wanted to get faster at drawing storyboards, so I practiced writing the text (alone) faster. If you find that's what slows you down, train by just writing back-and-forth conversations in list form.

More generally, you should analyze yourself. Polish the skills you have, and work on conquering your weaknesses as much as possible.

What are you mindful of when revising your own storyboards (either when self-editing or taking advice from editorial)?

Making sure the protagonist gets more panel time than anyone else. It's best to minimize parts that have nothing to do with your main character or the central plot. I'll even cut whole characters if they don't seem to advance the story.

When starting a storyboard, my goal is to tell the story I want to tell in the space I have, and not to be afraid of embarrassment.

The criticism from the editor may be brutal, but giving the storyboard your best effort is nothing to be ashamed of. Just take the critique and use it to improve next time.

Is there any way you could have been better prepared before your serialization began?

I never got to work as an assistant to a manga author, but I bet that would've been a great way to learn and pick up skills. Still, even without that experience, I had so many kind people willing to teach me things, so I guess it all worked out somehow.

What do you bear in mind when creating manga (e.g., personal themes and throughlines)?

Don't make simple concepts more complex than they have to be.

There have been so many instances where I've read a creative work filled with needlessly complex concepts and jargon. In those cases, I can never remember anything, I can't seem to understand what's going on (mostly because I'm a dummy), and I end up dropping whatever it is, which makes me so sad.

Continued...

What's your approach to creating strong, memorable characters?

I model characters on family, friends, and other real people in my life. Movies are also a source of inspiration, but I find that nothing beats real living, breathing people. I don't think it's great to rely solely on inspiration from other fictional works.

Try to analyze your own feelings about different people. What makes someone appealing? Or unbearable? Or worthy of respect?

How should one practice creating those strong characters?

A character is shaped by their origin, environment, personality, thoughts, words, and actions. Try to probe your characters' lives and values until you know them so well that they seem to take on life of their own, where you barely need to think about what they might say or do in any given situation.

How many works/pages did you create leading up to your first real submission? How many works/pages from that first submission until your magazine debut?

I've never been much for adding up numbers or math in general, so let's just say I created a lot.

What's your approach to creating manga that's readable?

Even if the world you're building is complex, don't try to explain it all right off the bat. Most readers will be overwhelmed if you inundate them with waves of unfamiliar terminology and tricky concepts. So keep it nice and simple—especially at the start—and appeal to the senses instead.

How long does it take to create the storyboards for a single nineteen-page chapter of manga?

Seven to ten hours.

How long does it take you to finish the full draft for a single nineteen-page chapter of manga?

About four to five days, probably.

Beyond creating your storyboards, what do you do to come up with ideas and plot points for your work?

I check out the newest and hottest works of fiction out there, and analyze them. Same goes for work by especially talented creators.

Is there anything you referenced when creating your one-shots?

I doubt I was able to make good use of my inspirations, but I've referenced old Japanese folktales, *Fujiko F. Fujio's SF Tanpen Theater*, *Parasyte*, and *Hissatsu Shigotonin*, among others.

SHUN SAEKI

[*Food Wars! Shokugeki no Soma*—ARTIST]

What knowledge would have benefited you when starting your manga career?

Having a complete and simple instruction manual (built into my head). I think all know-how about manga is valuable, so I really just wanted resources that could teach me everything, as I didn't have people in my life who could do that. Resources are so plentiful these days, so you have to sift through mountains of it all to find the good stuff (still, for most things, be sure to check out the reviews).

What did you do first after deciding to become a manga author [e.g., practicing, strategizing, etc.]? And/or, did you have an efficient way to practice?

Until my art started earning me money, I was the type to draw stuff aimlessly, without a thought in my head. It helped me polish my more alluring art, but that type of practice doesn't lead to overall growth, so I recommend drawing real things in real life. Nowadays, you have software like PureRef that provides reference images for just about anything you'd like to try drawing. Focus on that, and you'll get better by leaps and bounds.

What are you mindful of when revising your own storyboards [either when self-editing or taking advice from editorial]?

As an artist (and not a storywriter), this might not apply to me as much, but there have been times when a rough draft was sent back with things to fix. What I can say is this—it's really hard to remain completely objective about your own art, so waste no time in getting an editor or some other third party to give you feedback.

I understand having the occasional urge to scrap something you've done and fix it. But I'll tell you, something that's happened to me a lot is where some bit of art that I'm not crazy about or would even consider a failure somehow gets high praise from the fans and others involved. Or the opposite, where I'm really digging something I've done but it gets a lukewarm or chilly response. People's tastes are all attuned in different ways, so it almost feels like a waste of time to angst over something when you've only got your own feedback to go on.

Is there any way you could have been better prepared before your serialization began?

I was under the naive and mistaken impression that a *Jump* author's job can be summed up as "draw nineteen pages of manga per week." I wish I'd been prepared for the true scale of the workload (which goes far beyond a simple nineteen pages).

What do you bear in mind when creating manga [e.g., personal themes and throughlines]?

When I create art, I'm hoping to elicit straightforward and simple reactions from the readers. "Cool!" "Cute!" "Intriguing!"

Continued...

What's your approach to creating strong, memorable characters?

Artwise, I give each character little shticks. This comes in the form of facial expressions, gestures, and poses to strike.

How should one practice creating those strong characters?

My first move is to focus all my attention on crafting a character's basic facial structure, but it took me a while to realize that that isn't enough to make them appealing.

The facial expressions and movements (adding up to those shticks) are really key. You want to have an extensive library of options to choose from.

How many works/pages did you create leading up to your first real submission? How many works/pages from that first submission until your magazine debut?

Since I'm a perfectionist who gets hung up on details and will edit endlessly without ever finishing, I feel like I probably only had thirty or forty pages of completed manga before my first contest entry. Aside from tons of storyboards and doodles, of course.

I did lots of one-shots before getting serialized, so about five hundred or six hundred pages.

What's your approach to creating manga that's readable?

As an artist, I'd say "panel placement that makes the flow clear" and "good black/white balance." Most importantly, avoid art where it's unclear what's being portrayed.

How long does it take to create the storyboards for a single nineteen-page chapter of manga?

I couldn't say, since the storywriter handles that.

How long does it take you to finish the full draft for a single nineteen-page chapter of manga?

I finish a chapter in six days.

Beyond creating your storyboards, what do you do to come up with ideas and plot points for your work?

I always have TV shows or anime playing in the background while I work. And as mentioned before, I use that reference-image software called PureRef.

Is there anything you referenced when creating your one-shots?

I read so many first volumes of all sorts of manga series, for one.

KENTA SHINOHARA

[Sket Dance, Astra Lost in Space, WITCH WATCH]

What knowledge would have benefited you when starting your manga career?

Knowing how quickly hopeful manga authors finish off a completed draft. Starting out, it took me forever to draw just a single panel, so I couldn't help but wonder—does everyone else take just as long? Or am I literally the slowest person in existence?

What did you do first after deciding to become a manga author (e.g., practicing, strategizing, etc.)? And/or, did you have an efficient way to practice?

I started drawing storyboards. I don't remember setting aside specific chunks of time for practicing my art, so every time I hit a brick wall in the work, I guess I must've stopped and done some research to address the problem. That was my "practice."

Early on, my storyboards were full of detailed, deliberate art, so that must've helped me improve my art skills. Manga art can't reach its full potential if you avoid difficult perspective drawings and other things you're bad at, so it's best to force yourself to tackle your weaknesses head-on. You'll never improve enough to become a manga author if all you do is draw and doodle what you're good at, over and over.

What are you mindful of when revising your own storyboards (either when self-editing or taking advice from editorial)?

Take the phrase "But I already went to all this trouble..." and toss it in the garbage. Petty personal attachment can only get in the way, and the sunk cost fallacy will prevent real progress.

Is there any way you could have been better prepared before your serialization began?

You're better off having lots of ideas for scenes you want to draw. Even if the story's broader beats aren't solidified yet, having that stockpile of scenes to pick from will help move the plot along.

What do you bear in mind when creating manga (e.g., personal themes and throughlines)?

Readability. You might have a manga that controls the reader's rhythm just right, but if the reader is tripping over bits here and there, your carefully crafted tempo falls apart. In *manzai* comedy, they call this *kamu* [when the fast-talking performer gets tongue-tied and flubs a line]. This point applies to gag scenes, especially.

What's your approach to creating strong, memorable characters?

Some people will write up a whole character profile with details about appearance, personality, habits, a brief backstory, and so on, but I don't think that helps me create appealing characters. I don't really get a strong sense of my characters until I toss them into the manga and make them take

Continued...

action. When a series is heavy on the dialogue, especially, characters need to be paired up to see how they get along, how they interact, and so on. In those cases, I recommend creating a number of mock-up storyboards to better understand your own characters.

That said, for some authors, it is enough to create a profile sheet and be done with it. That depends entirely on the author, of course. Either way, the real trick is to make readers think, "I want to see more of this character."

How should one practice creating those strong characters?

In my early days, my editor gave me a homework assignment: "Think up one hundred characters that have nothing to do with your existing stories." Characters without existing roles in a story to give them context have to be appealing enough to stand on their own, so this felt like the purest way to practice the fundamentals of character creation. I recommend this method as well, since any decent characters you

come up with can then be waiting on standby for use in a future story. It was really tough for me, though. I quit after like fifteen characters.

How many works/pages did you create leading up to your first real submission?
How many works/pages from that first submission until your magazine debut?

I was twenty-eight or twenty-nine years old when I created my first real draft, and that ended up being the work I brought in to show an editor. The project that got serialized was my fifth overall.

What's your approach to creating manga that's readable?

Art, layout, word balloons. Drawings should be done carefully and deliberately. Use thick and thin lines where appropriate. Always be aware of the black/white balance. Good use of halftones keeps your art from being painfully bright.

Be sure to zoom the camera out for some panels (an annoying task, but it makes your manga more readable as a story when readers have a sense of characters' relative positions and distance).

Give every word balloon a tail so it's crystal clear who's talking. In panels with multiple characters and multiple word balloons, arrange all those components in a way that's easy to follow. When placing word balloons, always be aware that time is flowing from right to left and top to bottom. Only worry about techniques like leading the reader's eye once you've covered the above points and still have the leeway to arrange things further.

How long does it take to create the storyboards for a single nineteen-page chapter of manga?

For a weekly series, one chapter's storyboards take two days.

How long does it take you to finish the full draft for a single nineteen-page chapter of manga?

Again, for a weekly series, four days.

Beyond creating your storyboards, what do you do to come up with ideas and plot points for your work?

I jot down ideas I come up with using a phone app. When I come across an image that could inform my art, I save or download it. I think the advent of smartphones, the internet, and digital art tools is nothing but a positive for manga.

Is there anything you referenced when creating your one-shots?

Fujiko F. Fujio Sensei's *SF Tanpen Theater* were my bible. Just jam-packed with masterful storyboarding and clever use of ideas. It was instructive for me to witness how these legendary masterpieces were executed with shockingly low page counts.

My one-shot "Eikyuu Fumetsu Devil Point" was inspired by the sci-fi collection's "Mephisto's Ode to Calamity," while one of my shorter serializations, *Astra Lost in Space*, was inspired by "How to Build a Spaceship."

KAIU SHIRAI

[The Promised Neverland—STORYWRITER]

What did you do first after deciding to become a manga author (e.g., practicing, strategizing, etc.)? And/or, did you have an efficient way to practice?

I drew things from real life!

What are you mindful of when revising your own storyboards (either when self-editing or taking advice from editorial)?

What do I want to get across in this single chapter, and how do I want to captivate readers? Those are the essentials. Focus on fixes that bolster those factors.

For people who tend to overcorrect, shave away all other concerns that don't help you move forward.

If your problem is that you have trouble accepting tips and corrections from the editor, then once you've made the fixes, go back to your storyboard and think about what communication failure led the editor to make those comments.

Is there any way you could have been better prepared before your serialization began?

Having the ability to put together a chapter's worth of storyboards in just a week (or having the diligence).

(Those who do both story and art have to be even faster about it. Getting the storyboards done in one or two days puts you on solid footing.)

What do you bear in mind when creating manga (e.g., personal themes and throughlines)?

To create a product that reaches many people. Not one made out of complacency or self-satisfaction.

The latter route (that is, not thinking about the readers' perspective and only caring about your own enjoyment) has, at times, ended up producing decent stories, but it's not the approach for me. Whenever I stumble across a concept I find interesting, I start thinking about how to portray it in a way that others will enjoy as well.

What's your approach to creating strong, memorable characters?

The author has to have a clear understanding of each character's values and moral code. I have no hope of creating an appealing character if they haven't even taken proper shape in my own head. Then, I think about how to portray their values in an interesting way via their dialogue, their actions, and plot points that concern them. When I find a character intriguing but a reader doesn't, it's less often the case that my opinion was somehow wrong to start with, and much more likely that I simply failed to properly communicate what exactly is so great about this character. Characterization is a tricky thing to pull off that often leaves authors feeling lost, but the way I interpret the process is "Portray what feels like a real human being." I believe it was the director Akira Kurosawa who once said that.

How should one practice creating those strong characters?

Know what your characters are feeling and be sure to make that clear in every single chapter. I'm not great at characterization, actually, so please regard this advice as being the lowest possible bar to clear.

What's your approach to creating manga that's readable?

I identify what I want to communicate and transform that into a story organized in the best way possible for my message to come across.

I create storyboards that will be memorable even when skimmed. They need to have an engaging amount of variety, which comes from the rhythm, volume, and placement of dialogue; which bits of information are provided; page layout; page-turning motivation; and use of story beats.

How long does it take to create the storyboards for a single nineteen-page chapter of manga?

If I'm prepared to run myself ragged, then one week. Sometimes it's faster, and sometimes I can't possibly get it done within just seven days. I'm on the slow side. No doubt, being faster would be better.

Beyond creating your storyboards, what do you do to come up with ideas and plot points for your work?

When something genuinely speaks to me in daily life, I jot down a note about it. There's one unusual thing about my process, though. Rather than take those fun or interesting ideas and putting them in my manga as is, I tend to reflect on why I feel the way I do (about whatever it is) and then put that experience into the manga. That's what I'm better at communicating.

Is there anything you referenced when creating your one-shots?

No literature, really. Instead, I read every one-shot and *Weekly Shonen Jump* first chapter from the greats. I analyzed those stories and discovered that the climax (or turning point) was more effective when it came at the halfway mark, rather than the three-quarter mark, as one might expect. Little discoveries like that have stuck in my brain to this day.

HIDEAKI SORACHI

(Gin Tama)

What knowledge would have benefited you when starting your manga career?

We often see publicly available info about how pros with a team of assistants might split up their time and workload when trying to finish a draft, but you rarely see authors talk about doing all that work alone, despite the fact that that's the reality of it for most new authors. I think a lot of newcomers have their spirits crack under the weight of the overwhelming workload and end up giving up on their unfinished drafts. It would behoove them to hear a bit about the need to be mentally prepared for all that. My first-ever draft had me writhing in agony for half a year. The manga author's journey is at its most brutal right at the start.

What did you do first after deciding to become a manga author (e.g., practicing, strategizing, etc.)? And/or, did you have an efficient way to practice?

Introspection. I analyzed myself and reflected on my best weapons to take into battle (and my worst ones). I decided what I would set out to do (and what I wouldn't) with as much self-awareness as possible.

What are you mindful of when revising your own storyboards (either when self-editing or taking advice from editorial)?

I give my storyboards a fresh look and reexamine what role each page will play. For instance, one page might be the "free page" that comes before a big gag. So, which panels does it absolutely need, and which can it do without? I tend to have my metaphorical writer's camera pulled way back at first, but then I zoom in more and more until the details of the picture come into focus. That's the best way I've found to fix up my work.

Is there any way you could have been better prepared before your serialization began?

Having a stockpile of character designs to draw from in advance. Creating characters from scratch, while working on a weekly series? Woof, that's rough. Both mentally and physically.

What do you bear in mind when creating manga (e.g., personal themes and throughlines)?

I'm always searching for the intersection point of what I want to draw and what readers want to read. When there are lots of those intersections, that equals more opportunities to stop and take a breather. But if you only have one of those two lines to start with, you'll be caught up in one-way traffic and will just have to go with the flow.

What's your approach to creating strong, memorable characters?

I decide from the start what a given character is allowed to do and what they aren't, and make the character follow those rules to a T, at first. That's fundamental. If the author and reader don't have a basic shared understanding about the essence of a character, then by definition, the author can never do anything shocking or unexpected with the character to win them more fans. Next, create settings and stories that force you to loosen the rules that constrained your character.

Ultimately, I believe readers want to see characters acting like themselves at times, but also not, at other times.

How should one practice creating those strong characters?

When you find that you're fond of someone in life, analyze how your own feelings on them involved. Cases where you were a huge fan of someone from the start are less useful than experiences where you disliked someone at first and they ended up growing on you. For example, there might be some foul, disgusting creep of an actor who's obnoxiously handsome, but there come those rare moments when he says just the right thing on a variety show that makes you go, "Huh, he's not all bad." At that moment, drop what you're doing and run that self-analysis to figure out what's going on in your head. Why'd you hate him originally? What changed? As someone

creating characters, you have to be able to control that likable vs. unlikable dial however you see fit.

Continued...

How long does it take to create the storyboards for a single nineteen-page chapter of manga?

Three to five days.

How long does it take you to finish the full draft for a single nineteen-page chapter of manga?

Two to three days.

Beyond creating your storyboards, what do you do to come up with ideas and plot points for your work?

I consume lots of manga, movies, books, anime, and video games, I take note of story patterns and turn them into my personal stockpile of ideas. More specifically, I write down stuff I find interesting or boring, and then think about why I felt that way. It's my eternal homework assignment and hobby.

Is there anything you referenced when creating your one-shots?

My grand challenge was being more concise with my stories, so I read all the *Akamaru Jump** one-shots I could find and compared how each author approached their page distribution to my own approach, which helped me make progress. The tricks to cutting down on length are knowing when the scene changes should happen, knowing how long to spend on each scene, and cutting everything that can be cut.

*One of *Jump*'s older sister magazines. Now known as *Jump GIGA*.

RYUHEI TAMURA

(Beelzebub, Hard-Boiled Cop and Dolphin)

What knowledge would have benefited you when starting your manga career?

How to use correction fluid, since I didn't know that Misnon [a particular brand of correction fluid] even existed. Back then, when I screwed up, I'd have to scrap the whole page and start over. Every time, I'd think, "Man, manga authors have to have wills of steel to put up with this crazy work."

Guess I'm just one of those old fogies who the kids today can't relate to, with all their digital art options and whatnot...

What did you do first after deciding to become a manga author (e.g., practicing, strategizing, etc.)? And/or, did you have an efficient way to practice?

I think it's tremendously useful to get friends to read your stuff and provide feedback.

I was so eager for that feedback, though, that I would just pump out lots of storyboards done in pencil. It took me a long time to get used to pens and inking.

What are you mindful of when revising your own storyboards (either when self-editing or taking advice from editorial)?

I try to envision the me who drew the storyboards as a completely different person from the me who's going back to fix stuff. The first guy moves ahead at full steam, purely on instinct, while the second guy says, "Whoaaa there, buddy," and lives in the realm of logic and reason. I'm not the type to concern myself much with the plot, so at the stage when I'm just getting material onto the page, I'll find myself at a standstill if I aim for a high bar like "perfect" storyboards. Instead, I lower the bar (not always easy) and just get the work done. Then I can raise the bar again when it comes time to edit.

Is there any way you could have been better prepared before your serialization began?

Continued...

Having a bigger stockpile of usable characters would've saved my butt many a time. This becomes a more and more pressing issue the longer a series goes on.

What do you bear in mind when creating manga (e.g., personal themes and throughlines)?

A low threshold for entry and lots of laughs. Those are my guiding principles.

What's your approach to creating strong, memorable characters?

That humor element is a big one for me, personally. I have trouble drawing my characters (and liking them) if they're not funny. I'm just not well suited to villains and more serious characters. That's probably a sign that I need to challenge myself to change up my approach.

How should one practice creating those strong characters?

Throw multiple characters together, let them interact, and see how it turns out. Because a character is only as good as their interactions. It's hard to draw out a character's appeal when they're in a vacuum, all alone.

How many works/pages did you create leading up to your first real submission? How many works/pages from that first submission until your magazine debut?

My first thing that got into a magazine was my second major submission. Then I had three different one-shots, all leading up to my first serialization.

What's your approach to creating manga that's readable?

Bigger word balloons, less dialogue, five or fewer panels per page. That's ideal. I can't always stick to those rules.

How long does it take to create the storyboards for a single nineteen-page chapter of manga?

Three to four days. Lately I've been doing my own edits and drawings, which take a ton of time.

How long does it take you to finish the full draft for a single nineteen-page chapter of manga?

Four days. Three for inking the characters, and one more for finishing touches.

Beyond creating your storyboards, what do you do to come up with ideas and plot points for your work?

I consume media—TV shows, internet videos, radio, movies, dramas, anime. I also have my favorite media playing on a loop when I work, and somehow that helps me. The composition, the flow of dialogue, and things like that get drilled into my head.

Is there anything you referenced when creating your one-shots?

Short story collections and first volumes of serialized manga. In particular, referencing works that tell a complete story in just a handful of chapters is great for learning how to make the most of limited page real estate. I've read *Master Keaton* and *D-LIVE!!* so many times.

YUTO TSUKUDA

[Food Wars! Shokugeki no Soma—STORYWRITER]

What knowledge would have benefited you when starting your manga career?

I remember seeing "Use felt-tip pen or brush and ink for filling in black areas" written on the submission sheet and thinking, "What, I can't just use a brush pen?" That gave me some angst while doing my underdrawing. Luckily I had a pal who knew a lot about manga and told me that brush pen was fine. Phew.

What did you do first after deciding to become a manga author (e.g., practicing, strategizing, etc.)? And/or, did you have an efficient way to practice?

No special strategies, really. I made my serialized debut with storyboards that I drew while working a day job, so suffice it to say, I had no grand vision and was just sort of in a daze as it all happened... These days, I find it helpful to analyze the plots of existing manga when creating storyboards of my own.

What are you mindful of when revising your own storyboards (either when self-editing or taking advice from editorial)?

I feel like it's nearly impossible to look at my storyboards subjectively right after drawing them. I don't even attempt any self-editing; I just bring the work straight to my editor. Then I pit my opinions against theirs to decide how to fix things. For anyone who's considering submitting work and is about to dive down the rabbit hole of endless self-edits, I think there's something to be said for forgetting all that and just handing in what you've got.

Is there any way you could have been better prepared before your serialization began?

I might say something like, "I should've done more preliminary research," but the fact is, the research never ends once you're serialized anyway, so really, I've got nothing.

Continued...

What do you bear in mind when creating manga (e.g., personal themes and throughlines)?

I want the characters to create what feels like a place of belonging. In my own life, I'm happiest when I see characters in media and think, "Man, it would so *comfy* to hang out with those guys" or "I wish I could live in that world!"

What's your approach to creating strong, memorable characters?

Somehow making them feel human, warts and all. Fresh. Raw.

How should one practice creating those strong characters?

Ask yourself why your favorite characters are so appealing to you. Put serious thought into it, and put your answer into words. Then chat about it with friends and fellow authors. Once you're able to vocalize those thoughts and feelings, you can make use of that skill in manga.

How many works/pages did you create leading up to your first real submission? How many works/pages from that first submission until your magazine debut?

My first-ever draft (forty-five pages long) was a finalist for the monthly prize. My second work (thirty-one pages long) won the contest and ran in a sister magazine.

What's your approach to creating manga that's readable?

Keep your dialogue to only five lines of text (or less) per word balloon. Exceptions may apply.

How long does it take to create the storyboards for a single nineteen-page chapter of manga?

The first draft of my storyboards takes at least two days, possibly four or five if I don't have a handle on how my characters are thinking and feeling... Terribly sorry about those instances. Then I'll discuss with my editor before going back to the drawing board for a second draft, third draft, fourth draft, etc. My final product takes five to seven days.

How long does it take you to finish the full draft for a single nineteen-page chapter of manga?

With my old series, *Shonen Shikku*, about four days (my self-imposed quota was five pages per day).

Beyond creating your storyboards, what do you do to come up with ideas and plot points for your work?

When I heard that Yoshihiro Togashi Sensei had put together, on his own, a secret guide to help him with his own storyboards, I had to try that myself. I analyzed and compared existing stories, wrote down notes about them, and included tips and tricks about creating storyboards that I got from my editor and other authors. Oftentimes, when I come up against a brick wall, all it takes is a look at my secret notes to find the solution staring me in the face.

Is there anything you referenced when creating your one-shots?

I took a look at the one-shots in *Jump*'s sister magazine at the time, read them start to finish, and took note of how those authors handled their page distribution, for example.

TAISHI TSUTSUI

[We Never Learn]

What knowledge would have benefited you when starting your manga career?

I always wondered what sort of materials the pros used (pens, ink, correction fluid, paper, etc.). Here's what I use these days:

- Nikko's Nihonji Pen for characters
- a Nikko mapping nib for backgrounds and effect lines
- Pilot's black ink for drafting paper
- Misnon correction fluid
- I-C's 110 kg, B4-size draft paper

I'll do everything up through the line work with physical pen and paper, then scan in the work and add blacks and tones digitally in a program called Clip Studio. In the meantime, I'm training myself to eventually go full digital!

What did you do first after deciding to become a manga author (e.g., practicing, strategizing, etc.)? And/or, did you have an efficient way to practice?

When I really started drawing for real, I made a sketchbook out of a thousand pages of printer paper and set out to fill the entire thing in a month. Croquis drawings, sketches, doodles, you name it—the goal was to average thirty-four pages' worth of drawings per day.

It's questionable how effective this training was, but I feel like building up that sheer speed helped prepare me to endure the pace that a weekly series demands.

Hesitancy is another thing that affects how fast one can pump out finished drafts. I practiced telling myself, "Don't turn tail and run from compositions beyond your ability." Thanks to that training, I rarely find myself feeling lost or at a standstill with my underdrawings.

Finally, I examined my panel flow and the character dialogue of my favorite manga and copied it or referenced it to improve my own storyboarding.

Continued...

What are you mindful of when revising your own storyboards (either when self-editing or taking advice from editorial)?

It's essential to impose deadlines on yourself.

If you've got the leeway to edit and make little improvements, have a blast, but the worst-case scenario is not having a completed product in time. It's all a nonstarter if your work doesn't get finished. Working with an editor may give you additional wiggle room, but if you're on your own, you must have a clear understanding of how long it takes to create your storyboards and to revise them. Know how many pages you can pump out in one day, decide exactly when you're going to submit, and then stick to those quotas and deadlines like your life depends on it.

Is there any way you could have been better prepared before your serialization began?

Knowing how to create specification docs for requesting specific work from assistants. [*laughs*] Since before my weekly series, even, I'd been doing finishing touches digitally (and alone), so I had no clue about the workflow process when getting help from assistants.

I remember whining about the process after my weekly series began, so if you have any extra leeway at all, be sure to create those documents well in advance. It'll make instructing the assistants that much easier.

What do you bear in mind when creating manga (e.g., personal themes and throughlines)?

Above all else, I want readers to have fun and feel engaged by my work.

This is done not with dialogue, but by showing subtle emotions through scene layout, facial expressions, and the like.

Also, I usually try to hand in my stuff a week or more before the deadline (I've failed myself if my editor has to remind me about a deadline!).

What's your approach to creating strong, memorable characters?

This is a tricky one, but I often find myself wondering, "How can this side character contribute to the main character's appeal?"

The exact way a given side character achieves that helps guide that character's own characterization and informs their own appeal.

How should one practice creating those strong characters?

On the art side, when you see charming art, try copying it yourself and applying its charm to your own work. Study in detail what makes it so good, in your eyes.

For personality, write up storyboards and scenarios (even short ones) where you have your character taking action and speaking with lots of different characters. Do this until their essence starts to emerge, until you know exactly how this character reacts in a given situation. That understanding quickly helps them transform into a strong character.

How many works/pages did you create leading up to your first real submission? How many works/pages from that first submission until your magazine debut?

If we're talking my first published work in a magazine, I created quite a bit leading up to that point.

When I was a little kid, I penciled a few dozen "volumes" of manga in notebooks, but I got into the full-blown manga draft game pretty late. Rather than bring work to show professional editors, I put out a number of my own independent *dojinshi*-style pieces. Those *dojinshi* led

to a monthly serialization offer, and from there, I was lucky enough to get series in various magazines, all while learning the ins and outs of manga from editors and assistants while on the job.

Before getting into *Jump* proper, I'd had six different series running in monthly or biweekly magazines. Those amount to twenty-two volumes' worth of manga, which, at roughly 170 pages per volume, comes to about 3,700 pages. Add that to the *dojinshi* content and a handful of one-shots I did, and you get perhaps 4,000 pages total.

Probably best not to use me as a typical example...

What's your approach to creating manga that's readable?

- Give every character a distinct silhouette, so even in a long shot, it's obvious who's who.

- Keep page layout simple. Panels should remain within all the proper borders.

- Follow the 180-degree rule of film-making (e.g., a character on the right shouldn't suddenly be shown on the left).

- Make sure each word balloon has a tail pointed toward the speaker. When the speaker is off panel, add a little *chibi* drawing of the speaker's face (so it's still crystal clear).

- Don't allow the panel borders, word balloons, or other compositional elements to cut off parts of characters' heads or faces.

- Try not to have more than four lines of text per word balloon. Five at the absolute most.

Continued...

How long does it take to create the storyboards for a single nineteen-page chapter of manga?

Thirteen to fifteen hours. I'll start in the early afternoon on Friday and submit around 3:00 a.m. [Saturday morning].

How long does it take you to finish the full draft for a single nineteen-page chapter of manga?

I spend Saturday to Monday inking the characters. Then the assistants join me, and we spend Monday to Wednesday doing backgrounds and everything else (so I can submit on Wednesday).

About five days total.

Beyond creating your storyboards, what do you do to come up with ideas and plot points for your work?

I watch movies, read manga, etc. When something interesting comes up that I could make use of, I make note of it in an app on my phone, right there and then. Also, as I touched on before, when I find great art on the internet, I'll save the image, copy it by hand, and study what made it appeal to me in the first place.

Is there anything you referenced when creating your one-shots?

I've always been a big fan of Rumiko Takahashi Sensei, and I've looked back to her *Rumic World* story collection countless times.

POSUKA DEMIZU

(*The Promised Neverland*—ARTIST)

What knowledge would have benefited you when starting your manga career?

You can be a manga author without pulling all-nighters! And you don't have to develop calluses from holding pens! Even if you have a weak stomach, or are a slow learner, or don't have a high follower count, you can set out to do this job.

Fun fact: I grip my pen/pencil kind of weakly, so I don't have calluses. During my school days, I thought it would be cool to have calluses...so I tried rubbing my fingers a bunch to grow some. It didn't work. [*laughs*]

What did you do first after deciding to become a manga author (e.g., practicing, strategizing, etc.)? And/or, did you have an efficient way to practice?

Don't dwell on "Is this good or bad?" Just get the work done. Early on, when I was drawing manga with a pen, it took me one whole month to finish five pages.

Get the work done however you can, then show it to an editor. Friends and family might not give you the reaction you're hoping for, but an editor can point out what you've done well.

What are you mindful of when revising your own storyboards (either when self-editing or taking advice from editorial)?

It'll all work out, as long as your spirit doesn't break. Being motivated by deadlines can be a good thing. Enter every contest you can, for instance. If you endlessly revise, the work will never be finished. I tend to take the editor's advice most of the time, but I firmly believe that doing so (or not) is the author's choice (that didn't apply for me on *The Promised Neverland*, since Shirai Sensei did those storyboards).

Is there any way you could have been better prepared before your serialization began?

I wish I'd spent more time talking with friends and observing fun people. Thinking back, a lot of the characters I've created remind me of someone in real life, or wear clothing I've seen before somewhere, or say things that I've been told that really left an impression on me. A bigger stockpile to draw from can be super helpful later on.

What do you bear in mind when creating manga (e.g., personal themes and throughlines)?

Health comes first. Eat your meals, sleep at night, take walks. Also, try not to rely on nutritional supplement drinks... Save those for when your health is really going down the toilet.

What's your approach to creating strong, memorable characters?

Make every character instantly recognizable by their outward appearance alone! And not just

Continued...

via hairstyle or clothing. Maybe one character has big hands or big feet (a child with big feet will probably end up tall), or clear upper-body strength, or an interesting way of standing, or an especially high or low center of gravity, or little gestures they tend to do. Think about every aspect of the body when coming up with a character. Most of that even applies to nonhuman characters too.

How should one practice creating those strong characters?

Try showing off a wide range of characters; the result of that experiment amounts to practice.

Back in the day, I made up characters for fun and put them in mini manga stories on social media. Some of those characters were popular with my audience, while others came and went

without making a splash. I was thrilled when people liked a character enough to draw fan art, and that inspired me to create better and better characters.

How many works/pages did you create leading up to your first real submission? How many works/pages from that first submission until your magazine debut?

I don't remember! [*laughs*] During the ten-year gap between my first submission to *Jump* (during high school) and my first published work, I probably drew about one thousand pages of manga for various platforms.

What's your approach to creating manga that's readable?

Show people what you want to show them!

Emphasize those key elements visually and blur out or even omit the stuff that's just supposed to pass by without much notice. For every single panel, page, chapter, and volume, decide what elements you want to show most. That makes a manga readable.

How long does it take to create the storyboards for a single nineteen-page chapter of manga?

The underdrawing would take me two days (after Shirai Sensei did the storyboards). Up to that point, I would probably take three weeks to finish thirty pages of storyboarding on my own.

How long does it take you to finish the full draft for a single nineteen-page chapter of manga?

About six days! Two days for the underdrawing, two days for the line art, and two days for finishing!

Beyond creating your storyboards, what do you do to come up with ideas and plot points for your work?

For my background art, I like to use street view (on a digital map) to find and save images of buildings close to what I'm picturing in my head, so I'll often find myself checking out famous locations around the world and wandering around the map (so to speak). When I go out for walks in real life, I'll find interesting buildings, staircases, piping, and things like that, and take pictures.

Is there anything you referenced when creating your one-shots?

Talking with friends...I guess? I've often been given specific genres to work within, so I would talk with people who were savvy about those genres and find out what exactly drew them in! Now that I'm a proper adult, I guess I do the same thing, but with actual experts?

TATSUKI FUJIMOTO

[Fire Punch, Chainsaw Man]

What knowledge would have benefited you when starting your manga career?

I was working digitally, so I wish I'd known exactly how big a draft is supposed to be. I did my research on the internet and even trusted the info on Shueisha's official site, but that info turned out to be wrong! What a mess!

What did you do first after deciding to become a manga author (e.g., practicing, strategizing, etc.)? And/or, did you have an efficient way to practice?

Draw real stuff (dessin). Reproducing manga and anime by hand is more like an exercise for people who are already decent at art but need to figure out what good designs look like. So instead, I recommend drawing real people and places.

Also, you should always be thinking about what there is to be gained by drawing one thing or another.

What are you mindful of when revising your own storyboards (either when self-editing or taking advice from editorial)?

When I hit a stumbling block in the plot, I either alter the main character or scrap that bit of the plot entirely.

I understand why people get attached to their work, but if you spend all day every day staring at your own story, you're bound to lose that essential objectivity. Don't fall too in love with anything you do. Kill your darlings.

Is there any way you could have been better prepared before your serialization began?

Minding my health!

What do you bear in mind when creating manga (e.g., personal themes and throughlines)?

I try to create scenes that readers will remember until the day they gasp their dying breaths!

What's your approach to creating manga that's readable?

I take inspiration from people who might exist, who do exist, or who I might've seen somewhere! I'm not sure, really!

How should one practice creating those strong characters?

I never have!

How many works/pages did you create leading up to your first real submission? How many works/ pages from that first submission until your magazine debut?

Seven or eight different works, I think!

What's your approach to creating manga that's readable?

Keep the text and explanations to a minimum.

How long does it take to create the storyboards for a single nineteen-page chapter of manga?

One or two days!

How long does it take you to finish the full draft for a single nineteen-page chapter of manga?

Four to six days!

Beyond creating your storyboards, what do you do to come up with ideas and plot points for your work?

Nothing!

Is there anything you referenced when creating your one-shots?

I watched movies!

KOHEI HORIKOSHI

[My Hero Academia]

What knowledge would have benefited you when starting your manga career?

Knowing about perspective [in art] and human emotions.

What did you do first after deciding to become a manga author (e.g., practicing, strategizing, etc.)? And/or, did you have an efficient way to practice?

I started by reading a bunch of one-shots in *Akamaru Jump* and first chapters of various series. I analyzed them to see how many pages they needed to achieve good characterization, or how the chapters were split up in terms of setup, rising action, climax, conclusion, etc. Then, I systematically recorded all this data. I don't know how useful the data itself ended up being, but the act of breaking down published works like that deepened my understanding of manga as a medium, at least a little.

What are you mindful of when revising your own storyboards (either when self-editing or taking advice from editorial)?

I envision what it's going to be like when the chapter runs in the magazine. I have a keen awareness that it's going to be read, by real people. When the editor gives a suggestion I don't agree with, I push back and duke it out. Because nothing good can come of implementing a suggestion I just can't accept deep down. It wouldn't make sense.

Is there any way you could have been better prepared before your serialization began?

I could have been better prepared in *every way possible*.

What do you bear in mind when creating manga (e.g., personal themes and throughlines)?

How unsightly or awesome it can be when a character is covered in filth and struggling desperately. Having them rise up from that.

What's your approach to creating manga that's readable?

I wanted readers to have zero doubt about how much care and attention I pay to my characters. This usually comes in the form of the little details, like expressions, gestures, and so on.

How should one practice creating those strong characters?

There are times I've realized that *not drawing* something is the key.

For instance, say you have a character who's laughing out loud. You might make them roll around on the floor and kick their legs wildly, but those sorts of clichéd gestures are just default visual coding within the medium.

That isn't always *bad*, per se, but instead, try thinking about how your character, specifically, would act in that situation.

How many works/pages did you create leading up to your first real submission? How many works/pages from that first submission until your magazine debut?

Just one work, thirty-one pages long. The first manga I created was picked up. From there until my first serialization, I guess I had another one and a half series.

What's your approach to creating manga that's readable?

As a medium, manga is read by moving from one word balloon to the next, so

I'm careful about their placement.

Lately, I've been on a kick with close-ups.

How long does it take to create the storyboards for a single nineteen-page chapter of manga?

Two to three and a half days.

How long does it take you to finish the full draft for a single nineteen-page chapter of manga?

Four to five days.

Beyond creating your storyboards, what do you do to come up with ideas and plot points for your work?

Lots of doodling. As I'm drawing, ideas will pop into my head and/or crystallize into something usable.

Is there anything you referenced when creating your one-shots?

Akamaru Jump, and various first chapters.

YUSEI MATSUI

[*NEURO—Supernatural Detective,*
Assassination Classroom, The Elusive Samurai]

What knowledge would have benefited you when starting your manga career?

How to become a better artist. I'm sure that's a common answer.

I'm bad at summoning the effort to continuously produce art, so the only way to force myself to hone my skills was in the crucible of serialization. It took until my second series for people to stop calling me the worst manga artist around.

What did you do first after deciding to become a manga author (e.g., practicing, strategizing, etc.)? And/or, did you have an efficient way to practice?

Since I'm the type who can only make a real effort when it's do-or-die, my primary goal was simply to finish my drafts.

I would do my utmost not to lose interest partway through. I'd start with just three or six pages and *slowwwly* make my way from there.

At that stage, finishing the work in any form was a success story, and that's how I built up my confidence, little by little.

What are you mindful of when revising your own storyboards (either when self-editing or taking advice from editorial)?

Whether from myself or my editor, most of my revisions are along the lines of, "Something's lacking here—add more." Not so much, "You're going overboard here—pull back a little" (though that half of the equation does matter too). If you've got a storyboard packed to the gills with content, then when it comes time to tack on more, you'll have to delete something to make room. That can be tough.

As a result, I tend to leave about 10 percent of the storyboards' page count blank to start with. That makes the revision process a lot easier.

Is there any way you could have been better prepared before your serialization began?

Being savvier about instruction docs for assistants. I wish I'd been better prepared to instruct assistants on the basics of finishing my work, to tell them how to draw backgrounds appropriate for the story, and to provide them with reference materials.

I was decidedly unprepared for all that on my first series, so I had to take time to spell everything out for the assistants.

I also wish I'd had a stockpile of character designs, since there's so little time to start from scratch once a series is rolling.

What do you bear in mind when creating manga (e.g., personal themes and throughlines)?

I'm constantly striving to create something so worth reading that people will actually pay for it. Friends who look at my work for me, people who stand around reading the magazine in the convenience store without buying it, and those who read manga illegally on the internet are just *freeloaders* in my mind. But the people who open their pockets for my work are true *readers*, or even *valued customers*. There's a clear gap between those two camps, and if my hope is to satisfy the paying customers, then I can't afford to get complacent about my work.

What's your approach to creating strong, memorable characters?

As I see it, a strong character is one who comes into the lives of others and changes them for the better (especially mentally/emotionally). If you're not particularly accustomed to prioritizing characterization (I include myself in that camp), then don't start with the characters themselves. Start instead with what sort of effect or meaning they're going to bring to your world. Make them match the context of your story and world building, and it'll work out just fine.

How should one practice creating those strong characters?

I don't really have an answer for myself. I tend to prioritize all the other surrounding elements, because if those other elements are strong enough, then any character who slots perfectly into that setting will naturally wind up strong and appealing.

How many works/pages did you create leading up to your first real submission? How many works/pages from that first submission until your magazine debut?

I started drawing in my first year of high school. That period covered four distinct works and fifty pages over the course of four years.

Continued...

What's your approach to creating manga that's readable?

Pare down the text as much as possible. Bare-bones visual composition, outside of what needs to be shown. Avoid series-specific lingo and terminology. Always make it very clear, at any given moment, whether the reader should be focusing on the art or the story. Readability is a central pillar of making a manga succeed, so I try not to get careless about that fact.

How long does it take to create the storyboards for a single nineteen-page chapter of manga?

About three days for a serialization. But if I'm being honest and cut out all my time wasting, probably more like two days.

How long does it take you to finish the full draft for a single nineteen-page chapter of manga?

Two days for the underdrawing, then two more days for inking and finishing. That may make a lot of newcomers think, "No way...I could never!" But relax—the people who end up going crazy from the work don't have the foresight to ask this sort of question in the first place.

I will say, though, when it comes to a serialization, you have to get a sense of the moments when it's best to power through, and when it's better to take your foot off the gas.

Beyond creating your storyboards, what do you do to come up with ideas and plot points for your work?

I'm always strengthening my overall plots. Having a solid plot makes it so much easier to draw up storyboards.

First, I'll write up a loose list of future plot developments. Once I come up with specific story beats, scenes, and dialogue, I add them to the right spots in the narrative. I might build up a series of little moments until they become running gags. When enough of those details are in place, I bring them together to make a single chapter.

For my serialized series, I'll spend the Obon and New Year holidays holed up in a hotel room, plotting out the far-off beats of my story. During the beginning and middle of a series, I'll make adjustments along the way to ensure that readers stick with it, but the final arc will usually be set in stone, no diversions.

The final fifteen chapters of *NEURO* and the final fifty chapters of *Assassination Classroom* were like that. I had it all planned out to each chapter—each page, even—and in each case, I told the editor exactly what was coming down the pipeline.

Since the material is primed and ready to be made into storyboards, I'm then able to focus all my energy on the art and other minutiae. My life gets much easier at that stage.

Is there anything you referenced when creating your one-shots?

Since my goal was to make it into *Jump*, I made great use of *Jump*'s sister magazines, first chapters of *Jump* series, and collections of shorts from *Jump* authors.

KENTARO YABUKI

[To Love Ru series—ARTIST, Ayakashi Triangle]

What knowledge would have benefited you when starting your manga career?

Up to that point, I'd only ever drawn with pencils in notebooks, so when it came time to start doing real drafts, I had no idea what tools I needed or even where to buy them.

What's the right size for draft paper? How does one use tones properly? Do I draw the title logo myself? How do you insert dialogue right on top of the art, without a word balloon? Those sorts of things.

It was all stuff that you wouldn't find in a "how to draw manga" book. What I needed to know was much more fundamental than that.

What did you do first after deciding to become a manga author (e.g., practicing, strategizing, etc.)? And/or, did you have an efficient way to practice?

I focused on copying art from my favorite manga and anime series. I even attempted to draw some of that art from memory. Through enough of that practice, my own basic style began to emerge (mind you, I did this every day without fail starting in elementary school).

On the story-writing side, I would analyze one-shots and first chapters that I found particularly intriguing. I wrote down—in words—how these plots would flow, and I broke down the stories to see how many pages into the chapter a given development or twist would occur.

What are you mindful of when revising your own storyboards (either when self-editing or taking advice from editorial)?

I try to eliminate all unnecessary dialogue and panels. I find ways to give a character lines of dialogue and actions that only they are capable of. I lay the groundwork for those scenes that just scream, "Here's the highlight of the chapter!" Those are the major points I focus on.

It's important to me that whatever I'm drawing, I'm always having fun with it.

Is there any way you could have been better prepared before your serialization began?

Having more ideas for side characters [who interact with the main character] and villains.

Having that stockpile is essential. Even if you don't end up using a character at first, they're bound to come in handy down the line when you're swapping stuff around.

One's own life experiences are also key. In retrospect, I wish I'd explored and had more adventures during my teen years, to fill my mental library with more experiences to draw on.

What do you bear in mind when creating manga (e.g., personal themes and throughlines)?

I want my work to be pure entertainment. When a weary, exhausted reader sits down to enjoy my work, it should

Continued...

invade their brain and fill them with energy like some sort of nutritional supplement for the mind.

What's your approach to creating strong, memorable characters?

I'm conscious about finding the quickest and most efficient way to explain to readers, "They're *this* kind of character." A character's most evident traits and idiosyncrasies are tied to their overall appeal.

How should one practice creating those strong characters?

Make an effort to clear a space in your mind for the character to move in and get cozy. Chat with your family, friends, and editor about the character as much as possible and get them to ask you questions. You want to reach the point where your answers sound like, "Oh? Her? Yeah, when that happens, she responds like this!" as if this character is a real person you know.

Through this process, you'll come up against fewer roadblocks when storyboarding, because the characters will come alive and practically hand you their dialogue on a silver platter.

How many works/pages did you create leading up to your first real submission? How many works/pages from that first submission until your magazine debut?

My first submission got them to assign me a dedicated editor, and the second one (a one-shot) was published in a magazine. Then I got serialized. I consider myself extremely lucky that it only took me a

year and four months (after using real tools to create my first real draft) to get serialized. That said, my relative lack of experience came back to bite me in the period that followed.

What's your approach to creating manga that's readable?

Cut the fat and feature the minimum number of panels necessary. Use all the tricks to guide the reader's eye.

On the story side, you want every double-page spread to have one panel that's clearly the focal point (which is a separate matter from your overall climaxes).

Creating that tempo makes readers eager to keep turning the page.

How long does it take to create the storyboards for a single nineteen-page chapter of manga?

Nine to twelve hours. Chapters that feature a lot of fighting or sexy scenes get done even faster.

How long does it take you to finish the full draft for a single nineteen-page chapter of manga?

About thirty-nine hours of actual work, spread across five days.

Beyond creating your storyboards, what do you do to come up with ideas and plot points for your work?

I'm constantly thinking about manga, to the extent that one foot is always squarely planted in the world of my series. I randomly find myself thinking, "How would my main character go about this aspect of everyday life?"

I also have the TV, the radio, or YouTube playing in the background while I work. Anything that might provide ideas for content or bits of extra knowledge.

Lately, I've been listening to ghost stories. It's relevant to my story, of course, but I'm also studying the way these stories are constructed, and the way in which they dole out information.

When I'm browsing the net in search of material to help my art, I make a point of downloading art that instinctively makes me go, "Wow," or photos shot at strange angles that could be difficult to draw.

Is there anything you referenced when creating your one-shots?

I personally found the *Rurouni Kenshin* one-shot to be amazing, and I referenced it as my platonic ideal.

Beyond that, I read as many one-shots and first chapters as I could get my hands on. Then, when I moved to Tokyo, Kazuhiko Torishima* invited me to a conference room at Shueisha, sat me down (just the two of us), and told me that the first chapters of both *Slam Dunk* and *Fist of the North Star* are perfect masterpieces of the craft. Following his advice, I bought those two books and analyzed them in detail.

*The editor in chief of *Weekly Shonen Jump* at the time.

CHAPTER 4

WHEN STUCK, RETURN TO YOUR FOUNDATION

After Saito sent Kosei the survey answers from the *Jump* authors, the boy dropped out of touch for a while. Saito couldn't help but wonder how Kosei was doing, but then, when grabbing lunch at a restaurant one day, he ran into a familiar face staring at some blank notebook pages.

■ What do I do when I keep rejecting my own ideas and can't seem to progress?

SAITO: Well, if it isn't Kosei! We haven't heard from you in a while. Did you happen to read through those survey answers?

KOSEI: Huh? Oh. It's you, Mr. Saito. Sorry for not keeping in touch. I forgot to thank you for sending me that stuff...

SAITO: I was just wondering what you might be up to. Ah, this is my boss from work, Asada.

ASADA: Hey there. I'm Asada. I work over at Shueisha with Saito here.

SAITO: This is Kosei, the high schooler who brought in some art samples.

KOSEI: *Th-the* Mr. Asada! I've seen your name in interviews and stuff, sir. You were the first editor assigned to big hits like *One Piece* and *Bleach*, right? You're basically a legend as far as manga editors go...

SAITO: Don't get starstruck on us, now! But since we're here, why not have a chat? Can we take a seat at your table?

KOSEI: What? I could never... I mean, I'm sure you guys have places to be, stuff to do!

ASADA: Don't sweat it. We're already here for a meal, aren't we? Say, have you been drawing manga in that notebook?

KOSEI: I wish...

See, I read through those survey answers you sent me, and I mean, wow. You've got Horikoshi Sensei, who got published in a magazine after creating just a single one-shot, or Tsutsui Sensei, who went around drawing thirty-four pages' worth of art every single day! Those guys are total beasts. When I realized I could never hope to get on their level, I just kinda froze up. Whenever I try drawing now, I start thinking I'll never get a series in a weekly magazine. **Nothing I draw is ever gonna be good enough.**

SAITO: I was hoping that it would motivate you to learn that even the pros had their struggles and needed to practice a lot before making it big. Sorry to hear that it had the opposite effect.

KOSEI: I guess it just opened my eyes up to reality? I can tell that these *Jump* authors exist on another plane of talent altogether...and that kinda put me in a funk.

ASADA: Lemme ask you this, then—does any part of you still want to create manga?

KOSEI: Sure, there's lots of stuff I wanna draw...but it's hard to imagine ever going pro.

ASADA: Then keep at it. The pros often say that **nothing good can come of self-rejection.** Put in the time and work, and you're sure to improve. **Rather than creating a long hundred-page story, trying for four stories that are twenty-five pages each will help you grow more.** I got no solid proof—just my own experience—but I say your manga skills will be honed with each story you put to paper, start to finish.

SAITO: That's just another reason why I recommended creating a number of shorter works.

KOSEI: But when you've only got a few dozen pages for a one-shot, it's hard to tell a complete story.

■ An idea I've had forever just isn't coming together. Should I abandon it?

ASADA: So these are ideas you've had for a while? But they're just not coming together, no matter what you try?

KOSEI: Yeah, one idea is for this battle scene. And the rest, well, I've drawn less than two pages.

ASADA: Then think up something else for your practice one-shot. You froze up because your head's bursting with more ideas than it knows what to do with. **Start by drawing what you can, and what you know.** Model your characters on real people, like friends or teachers. You could even ask an editor like Saito for a specific prompt.

SAITO: One of *Jump*'s newcomer contests, Story King, specifies a genre and provides a prompt because many manga hopefuls find that approach easier to tackle. Plenty of young artists will narrow down their concepts even further. Something really simple, like "bathing suit" or "glasses." Why not give that a try?

KOSEI: Right. In those survey answers, the pros said stuff like, "**Just finish as many works as you can**" or "**Make your own deadlines and stick to them.**" I guess I've been too fixated on a few specific ideas to really move ahead. But the thing is...

■ Unfavorable comparisons left me traumatized, and now I'm scared to ask for feedback...

KOSEI: Is there any point to finishing a story if what I really want to draw just isn't good enough?

SAITO: Instead of taking that attitude, bring your work to an editor to receive feedback. Because it's true—you'll never complete anything if you're thinking, "What's even the point of showing anyone when I'm not happy with how the work turned out?" That's just you erecting more hurdles inside your own mind. Instead of letting it come to that, keep drawing every day. Even the shortest of short stories. **Make manga about your daily life, like what you had for breakfast, or the start of a movie you saw, or a video game you played.**

ASADA: And if the thought of getting feedback is scaring you into submission, then draw something that you've got no intention of showing anyone at all. Even if it's just a scrap of a scene that's been on your mind because it seems cool, or gruesome, or somber.

KOSEI: Right... Actually, I posted some of my one-page and two-page manga samples on Twitter and got, like, zero engagement. And these were the good ones! Then I showed some of my manga to some friends for the first time and asked them what they thought was missing. You know what they gave me? Brutal honesty, emphasis on "brutal." Kicked the ever-loving crap outta my work. It kinda broke my spirit.

SAITO: I'm guessing that hurt even more than reading the two-page samples from the pros and going through their survey answers?

KOSEI: I mean, for sure. It all combined into a one-two-*three* punch. A big pile-on.

ASADA: Try asking folks what they like about your work, instead of what's lacking. Find people who are willing to prop you up while still being honest. A professional editor would be best. Nothing wrong with having family and friends look at your stuff, but when the ones doing the reviewing aren't exactly your target demo, their advice can often go in bad directions.

KOSEI: Um, a target demo...?

ASADA: All I mean by that is the sort of folks you're imagining will be reading your work once you're successful. Find people who fit that image. A huge chunk of the feedback you're gonna see on the internet or from people on the street is limited to "I like series X" or "I don't like series X." Their judgments don't really extend past that. Meanwhile, editors have a way of envisioning an author's "final form," so to speak, and asking themselves, "How's this talent gonna grow?"

■ Being compared to others makes me doubt myself. How do I deal with those feelings?

KOSEI: Another problem is, whenever I start comparing myself to other artists and authors, it feels like I'm way outta my league.

ASADA: Those comparisons are a fact of life. Once upon a time, before the days of the internet, a kid might've thought he'd be a manga author someday since he was the best artist in his class at school, but now we've got pixiv, Twitter, and what have you. Having instant access to a whole world of talent tells that same kid that he's not king of the mountain—just his little molehill. A powerful sense of confidence can still work wonders for the right person, but these days, it's much easier to lose hope and wither on the vine. Tough times, I say.

KOSEI: Before I started drawing, I was like, "Yeah, I bet can I draw!" Then I started, and it was like, "Just kidding, I suck at this!" Seeing all these pro artists on the internet and the pages of *Jump* is like another harsh reality check...

ASADA: You're not the first person to feel like they can't do it, you know? But you've still got goals in mind, right? Somewhere, deep down, you've got strengths waiting to be found, so let's search for them together.

SAITO: This is why I keep recommending that you work with an editor. If I don't seem like the right fit for you, then we'll find you someone who is. Also, start something like a daily manga journal. A little world of your own, where you can draw every day without any external input or interference. These things will go a long way toward giving you stability and peace of mind, which are conducive to improvement.

■ The thought of showing my work to an editor is scary. Can't I just upload it to social media?

ASADA: Some manga hopefuls find it too taxing to meet up with editors and opt for uploading their work on social media instead. And that's fair enough. I gotta warn you, though—all those likes and retweets and whatnot may be your audience telling you they wanna see more, but don't mistake that for a willingness to open their wallets to buy books at a store. And while plenty of authors are fond of self-promoting and posting their stuff on social media, there are still plenty of big shots who don't dabble with that at all, so if playing the social media game isn't your thing, don't sweat it. I'll also mention that it's still rare to find a long-form manga posted on social media that's selling as well as the series in *Jump*. Each platform's generally got a certain type of manga that tends to do well in that arena, so depending on what kind of manga you're making at the moment, the social media approach might be the right fit, or it might not. Anyhow, sorry for getting off track there.

KOSEI: Well, I've always had my eye on *Jump*, so...working with an editor is probably the way to go.

■ How do I pick myself back up when my spirit is crushed?

KOSEI: When my confidence is down the drain and I've lost sight of what makes me, me...what do I even do?

ASADA: How about going back to your starting point? Your origin? When *My Hero Academia* author Horikoshi Sensei saw his previous series end, he decided to take another look at a one-shot from his newcomer days called *My Hero*—a piece of work he felt attached to and that had come very naturally to him. He took some of the elements from that story and wound up expanding them into the series we now know as *My Hero Academia*.

SAITO: "Up against a wall? Head back to your origin." That's a concept that sometimes comes up in editorial talks. When people are caught up in the hustle and bustle of their careers, they can wind up with big heads or lose their way entirely. Especially when they experience setbacks or failures and then have to bear witness to the successes of others. It's easy to lose confidence.

ASADA: Sometimes an author won't end up doing what they're suited to because they think things like, "I wanna follow in the footsteps of some popular series that sold great" or "I'd like to create a series that garners nothing but the highest praise from all." Those notions can be huge distractions. **The question you should ask yourself is, "At the end of the day, what do I want to create more than anything else?"**

KOSEI: Hey, that sounds like the first bit of advice Mr. Saito ever gave me. And y'know, I did go and have those chats about manga with friends who are into the same stuff...right up until they trashed my work and put me in a funk. Those convos were fun and all, but I dunno if they really helped me figure out what I want to create. The answer to that question's still kinda fuzzy for me.

ASADA: Maybe you just haven't read enough yet? Keep on picking up books—even genres you haven't so much as glanced at—and try to work out why the good ones grab your interest and the others don't. Don't limit yourself to manga either. Read novels, listen to music, watch movies, browse videos on YouTube. Looking inward can only get you so far without a healthy dose of media to consume, analyze, and dissect in your own words. When you come across a piece of media you hate with a fiery passion? Man, consider yourself lucky. Because the flip side of that realization is the chance to think about how you could've done it better. That's why editors always have lots of recommended reading for the authors they work with. **Having a clear sense of your own likes and dislikes is a natural route to piecing together what it is you want to create**, even if it's as simple as you thinking, "This bit of art is just awesome!" That's when you start doodling. Not everything you do has to be some act of pure, divine creation, like a piece of your soul you've ripped out and put on the page. When you see a photo or drawing that makes you go. "Cool scene!" or "Cute costume! or "Clever composition!" just get out the pen and do some doodling of your own. Turn your characters into *chibi* versions. Swap their genders around. Put them in a different historical period. By getting your drawing hand moving and having fun with it, your own tendencies and specialties are gonna come into view before you know it.

SAITO: Some authors I know make a point of watching a lot of boring, awful movies to the bitter end. That allows them to develop that all-important sense of, "How would I do this instead?" You don't necessarily have to go that far, but I'll stand by the idea that **it's to every author's benefit to nail down their artistic values as soon as possible**.

■ I'm not sure what makes a series sell. I don't have the instincts for marketing.

KOSEI: They always say it's bad to be a picky eater, or to prefer certain school subjects over others, but you're saying it's important for a manga author to have strong preferences? Honestly, I don't have a real sense for what makes a series sell well, so I'm worried that my instinct for these things is out of whack.

ASADA: Here's an example. I'm a fan of this old baseball story that ran in *Jump* called *Forever Shinji-kun*, by Katsuyuki Edamatsu Sensei. That series ran for all of three volumes and couldn't be called a commercial success by any standard, but man, I loved that series like nothing else at the time, and nobody could tell me otherwise.

SAITO: On the other hand, even the biggest megahits are going to turn some people off, which is totally normal. Nothing's forcing you to make your own tastes conform to what's considered mainstream, and when it comes to your own work, always remember that you can't win over everyone all the time. Being an avid people pleaser rarely ends well.

ASADA: If you're gonna go about taking inspiration from the big hits, make a habit of really zooming in and figuring out what makes them tick. Gotouge Sensei mentioned something like that in those survey answers, yeah? During my one-on-ones, I like to ask authors, "What'd you think of *Jump* this week?" or "What worked so well about this one-shot?" Stuff like that. Back when I was the editor on *One Piece*, Oda Sensei and I would chat about *Hikaru no Go* (by Yumi Hotta Sensei and Takeshi Obata Sensei). Making a manga series for kids that focuses on the game of go sounds like an uphill challenge, right? So how'd the authors do it? I'd ask Oda Sensei what he thought about the way they implemented certain ideas, or why one part or the other turned out so fun.

SAITO: Having these conversations with someone else can also bring to light how your tastes may differ from theirs. It'll help you put your thoughts into words and elaborate on your own ideas, more so than sitting and thinking by your lonesome.

KOSEI: So... I need to return to my origin, figure out my tastes and preferences, and talk them out with other people... Got it.

■ Why aren't the parts I worked on the hardest the parts that people praise?

ASADA: One more thing. When you're having trouble judging the quality of your own stuff, trust what other people are telling you. **Your greatest weapon might be one you never noticed before.**

KOSEI: Okay! Actually, I don't get that part...

SAITO: For example, say you're telling everyone that you'd like to create an action series, but for as long as anyone can remember, your drawings of cute girls have been imbued with clear passion. That might actually be your secret weapon.

ASADA: Some authors do better with series full of boys, and others tend to hit it big with series focused on girls. Sometimes that tendency doesn't necessarily match up with the author's stated goals. Who knows? Maybe you're the kinda guy who'd be better off drawing women?

KOSEI: Can't say I hate the idea of drawing girls, but writing a romantic comedy? Nah, I'd be dying of embarrassment the whole time.

SAITO: There are more than a few authors who happen to excel at exactly the type of content that makes them cringe, or that they would naturally shy away from doing for whatever reason. At first, they're scared that people in their lives might mock them or otherwise question what they're doing, but sometimes all it takes is a simple "Wow, this might be what you're suited to?" to clear away the doubt and unlock this hidden talent.

ASADA: In the survey answers, Akutami Sensei said, "I'm not trying to get people from my own generation to come away thinking I have good taste." That's in the same vein as what we're saying. Instead of putting on a performance for some imagined audience, let your freak flag fly.

■ How do I find a compromise between the content I want to create and the demands of the readers?

KOSEI: Hang on a second... You've been telling me all along to "draw what I like," so I'm feeling like there's a contradiction here.

ASADA: It's tough to explain. Lots of authors will have three different answers to "What do I want to do?" "What am I suited to?" and "What does the audience want?" Sometimes, those three answers overlap perfectly, which is ideal, but even the authors who make it into *Jump*

have to make compromises between what they want and what's feasible. Mostly because *Jump* demands those relatively short nineteen-page chapters every week, with tight deadlines.

KOSEI: So finding that overlap between what I want to do and what I'm good at isn't even enough? You're saying the specific magazine comes with all these other limitations, and the author has to make more compromises around that? Sheesh, that's a lot...

ASADA: Authors tend to prioritize their own wants, which is just fine at the start. But accepting those external demands can actually be another way to grow and improve.

KOSEI: I'm sorry. You've totally lost me now. What am I supposed to do? I don't really understand.

SAITO: At first, you **draw what you love**. Then there'll come a moment when you have to make a shift and cater to your audience more. That stage will involve plenty of trial and error as you make adjustments to compromise between your own wants and the demands of the readers. The distinction is not to focus on catering to anyone else while you're still discovering your own taste. That's a great way to end up lost, without a real identity. **You start with what you want in order to create that rock-solid foundation**. Once all the cornerstones are set in place, you can begin construction that addresses the external demands. There's an order to those two stages—they can't both happen at once.

KOSEI: Hmm, I hear you. Well, this talk motivated me to get back to the drawing board as soon as I can. Once I've figured out what I'm doing a little more, I'll get in touch again!

CHAPTER 4 KEY POINTS

- When you find yourself unable to draw, you may be trying to include too much content all at once. Try narrowing down the scope until it feels more manageable.

- The more complete stories you finish, the more you'll improve. Instead of saddling yourself with a long-form work, try pumping out a number of shorter stories.

- When comparing yourself to other authors has stripped you of your confidence, or when too much criticism has left you reluctant to show others your work, don't force yourself to relive that trauma. Draw what you like as a form of rehab.

- Talk to people who can look at a story and envision its future. They can tell you how the story might grow and evolve, instead of focusing on the more basic matter of present quality. You want conversation partners who can point out the strengths of a given work, and not just the flaws. An editor is your best bet.

- Rather than brooding alone, talking to others can help the ideas flow and grow.

- Many people have a hard time recognizing their own greatest weapons. Let compliments from others inform you and give you confidence. Explore the idea of working with content that at first makes you think, "Drawing that would be mortifying!" You might unexpectedly strike gold.

- There comes a time in a professional's career when they must shift from creating solely what they love to making content that's more audience oriented. When that point arrives, a successful author will use their own tastes and preferences as the foundation to build their work to meet the demands of the readers.

TRY IT OUT

▷ Don't focus only on content you want to draw. Expand into more diverse subject matter that you're capable of creating.

▷ When feeling lost, return to your starting point. Toss aside all secondary concerns and remind yourself exactly what it is you love to create.

▷ Within everyday life, get used to explaining in words what you like or dislike, and why. This process may provide valuable insights when it comes time to create.

▷ Speak to a trusted friend about why a certain piece of media appeals to them so much (or why it doesn't). Make use of those conversations when it comes time to grapple with your own work.

FREQUENTLY ASKED QUESTIONS FROM NEW AUTHORS

PART 2

Q2

My story doesn't end conclusively, like most one-shots. Can I give it a vague "To be continued..." ending, as if it were the start of a serialization?

A

This may sound harsh, but no—don't take the easy way out and resort to a fake "To be continued..." ending just because you couldn't wrap up your story properly. Ending stories is a valuable skill that will help you grow as an author.

If your process isn't going well, stop overcomplicating the matter and boil it down to three key elements: ① **a protagonist**, ② **the protagonist's actions**, and ③ **the changes that the protagonist and the world around them have undergone between the first page and the final one**. Define those elements clearly and focus on them.

Often, the root cause of a story's failure to wrap up cleanly is an author who's unwilling to shave away and make appropriate cuts. But that determination is misdirected. Harden your heart, write up a priority list, and kill your darlings. At all times, imagine yourself as a reader. Has any story with a half-hearted sputter of an ending ever made you think, "Wow, that was fantastic!"? Being able to straddle the creator/reader mindset will get you one step closer to pro status.

TADAHIRO MIURA SENSEI'S TIPS FOR DIGITAL ARTISTRY!

With a new outlook on the craft, Kosei is finally getting the hang of drawing manga. Now he's eager to try working digitally but has no idea where to begin. At Saito's suggestion, Kosei has a chat with Tadahiro Miura Sensei (known for *Yuuna and the Haunted Hot Springs*) about how to bring his visions to life with the proper technology and digital tools.

■ What's the best way to start making manga digitally?

MIURA: Hi there, I'm Tadahiro Miura.

KOSEI: N-nice to meet you, sir! So, the thing is, I've only worked with analog tools so far, but the other day, a friend let me mess around with Clip Studio Paint on their computer, and it seems like a fun way to go about making manga. When I told Mr. Saito I wanted to dabble in digital, he was nice enough to set up this meeting. Anyway, sorry—I'm super excited to meet a pro manga author for the first time and I love the way you draw cute girls, so I'm kinda all nerves over here at the momenphth! Ack, bit my tongue there...

SAITO: D-dial it back, Kosei.

KOSEI: Yeah, thorry...

SAITO: In any case, Miura Sensei, we know that you're so well versed in Clip Studio Paint that other pros often come to you for advice about making manga digitally. Plus, *Jump*'s manga contests receive more and more digital entries lately, since one can submit directly via the official websites, so Kosei here certainly isn't the first manga author hopeful to ask me about these things. "Analog or digital?" is just as common a question as "What sort of manga should I create?" On that note, Sensei, I'd be grateful if you could answer Kosei's questions today.

MIURA: Absolutely. Ask away!

■ Which is better—a pen tablet or a pen display? How do I avoid picking the wrong device?

KOSEI: Let's go ahead and assume I'm a total newbie who wants to know the most basic of basics about these devices... When it comes to making manga, which is better—a pen tablet or a pen display?

The information about digital art in this chapter is just a small fraction of what there is to know about Clip Studio Paint as of April 2021. Be sure to consult the software's manual or online user guide for more details.

MIURA: Both can get the job done, but for someone starting out, I'd recommend the pen display. It's easier to work with since, of the two, it's the closest experience to drawing on actual paper.

SAITO: Newcomers often come to me with concerns about this technology. Some tell me that trying to draw on a laptop—as opposed to a desktop—makes their machines chug from lack of processing power. Others tell me that the larger pen displays will overheat, forcing them to wear long sleeves if they don't want to burn themselves, especially in the summertime. And still others wonder what size pen tablets to buy for this sort of work. Do you have any advice about picking just the right device?

KOSEI: Yeah, all that! What he said! These things aren't cheap, so I'm gonna be hurting if I shell out for one and then realize I can't even use it properly...

MIURA: It's true, there's a lot that can go wrong. Even the newest tech from the leading brands—which can cost a few thousand bucks—can have batteries that bulge or screens that crack and peel off.

KOSEI: Yikes!

MIURA: To avoid that kind of costly malfunction, I say you're better off picking a model that's a few years old, with plenty of good reviews from users. That's the safest bet.

SAITO: So it's safer not to opt for the newest technology on the market, then.

MIURA: As for the matter of a computer's processing power, I recommend the build-to-order method where you customize your PC before it ships. That way, you can choose the exact specifications recommend by software like CSP.

SAITO: What about the pen displays that overheat?

MIURA: That can be unavoidable, so just try to work in an air-conditioned room. And when it comes to tablet size, that's more a matter of personal preference. I've tested just about every size, from biggest to smallest, and eventually settled on the fifteen- or sixteen-inch models. That said, many artists I know are so used to working with B4-size draft paper that they prefer larger tablets, around twenty inches and above.

■ How do I properly back up my data?

KOSEI: Is there any special tech that only the pros have? Stuff that makes you say, "Wow, this is handy"?

MIURA: My leading candidate would have to be any sort of left-hand device, like a keypad for the hand that's not busy drawing. It's useful to program those with shortcut commands—though your mileage may vary, and it's hardly an essential piece of tech. Ah, one more thing. It's not something that every pro uses, but I definitely recommend using NAS.

KOSEI: Wuzzat?

MIURA: Short for "network attached storage," it's a hard drive for storage that's accessed over a network. Just like art made with pen and paper, your digital art data could be lost due to any number of problems. Your PC or external drive might break, you might lose internet access, the cloud might malfunction, or your files might get deleted thanks to simple human error. Fun fact—I've experienced every disaster I just mentioned.

KOSEI: Yeesh... It's that easy for technology to fail, huh?

MIURA: It's definitely risky to only have your data stored in a single place. That's why you want NAS that syncs with cloud storage. Personally, I use the group work function of CSP, and those particular art files are stored locally on mine and my assistants' computers, as well as on the NAS and the cloud. That way, the exact same data always exists in at least three different places at any given time, so unless we have three independent tech failures all at once, the work will be safe. When starting out, though, I think an online storage option like Dropbox is probably good enough. Not too many authors I know use NAS, though most go for some kind of cloud storage.

KOSEI: The pros take lots of cautionary measures, I guess.

MIURA: I also keep a portable generator around in case of blackouts, because it takes something pretty apocalyptic to warrant an extension of your deadlines. Even in the wake of the Great East Japan Earthquake disaster of 2011, I was told I'd only get an extra week to finish my one-shot...and even that ended up being a lie. They still refused to shift the deadline.

KOSEI: You gotta be kidding me! Hang on, is that true, Mr. Saito?

SAITO: Everything was so up in the air during that period, changing from one minute to the next...

MIURA: A pro has to be prepared to expect the unexpected and adapt.

When creating digital art, how do I set the correct canvas size?

SAITO: Regarding the proper draft paper size for manga... Different sources provide slightly different information. And the digital canvas setting in CSP has its trim line in a different spot than physical Japanese draft paper. Not to mention, paper size varies depending on whether you're talking about a magazine or a compiled volume. With all that in mind, I'm often asked how to get the canvas size just right when drawing digitally.

MIURA: If it's a matter of the exact dimensions, CSP actually has a number of presets for different magazines, including *Weekly Shonen Jump*. That's the easiest way to be sure. When starting a new project, that's accessed via "Show All Comic Settings" from the "Use of Work" options. The list of available presets should include the following option:

Shueisha manga A *(e.g., Shonen Jump, Margaret)*

Using that preset provides you with all the proper margins for publication in a magazine. For a volume edition, everything you draw up to the top edge would be printed.

KOSEI: I'll start practicing with that preset, then!

MIURA: That same preset even includes the option for a safety margin. When your word balloons and essential art just have to burst beyond the standard border, employing that safety margin ensures that you won't lose anything critical when the work is cropped for a magazine or volume. Personally, I think it feels good to use that technique occasionally. Still, you're typically better off not pushing the envelope like that.

KOSEI: How would I go about doing a double-page spread in CSP?

MIURA: From the "Page Manager" window, pick either the left or right page you want to turn into a double-page spread, right click, and from the pop-up menu, select "Combine Pages..." Then, check "Merge Margins TBD" and click "Okay" for the "Gutter TBD" being set at -9.6 mm.

SAITO: There's also a slight size difference between the magazine and published volumes, so be sure to pass along your work to your editor at the underdrawing stage so they can check with the print shop and be doubly sure.

■ What are some tips and things to look out for when polishing my saturated lines and hand-drawn lettering?

SAITO: A big advantage of digital is having total command over saturated lines and hand-drawn lettering. Miura Sensei, do you have any tips or things to look out for when it comes to those?

MIURA: I don't personally use the "Saturated Line" tool. Instead, I opt for the "Radial Line Ruler" and draw my lines individually with the pen. I'll also say that I don't use the typical pen setting for saturated lines, since the thickness changes depending on pen pressure. Those sorts of special effect lines should have uniform thickness at the starting point, so you'll want to turn off pen pressure and check the "Ending" box to have your lines taper at the endpoints.

KOSEI: Sure, I think I get it. What about hand-drawn lettering and sea urchin flashes, those spiky balloons?

MIURA: For that hand-drawn look, you could create your own calligraphy-like brush tool, or use word balloons to make bubble lettering (characters made up solely of outlines). CSP provides a wide variety of materials for hand-drawn lettering, so you can use your favorites while developing your own self-made options. If you need lettering with a white outline (that stands out more against the background), just activate "Border Effect" in the "Layer Property" palette to add those outlines automatically, with adjustable thickness. As far as sea urchin flashes go, you can create your own with the "Saturated Line" tool and save your creations to the material palette to use whenever you want.

KOSEI: Wow, that really is handy!

MATERIAL PALETTE   This is an example of one way that the Material Palette looks! Yours will have a different look of its own, as you customize and create your own balloons and assets.

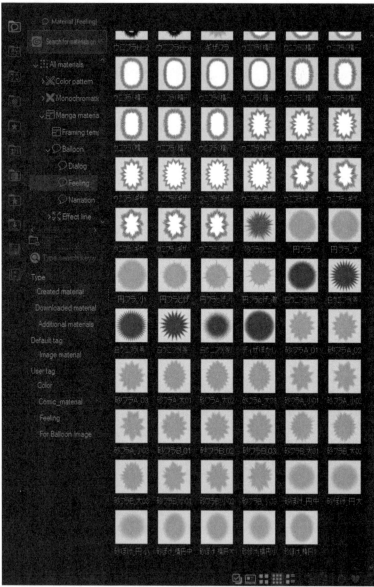

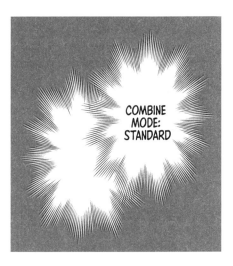

COMBINE
MODE:
STANDARD

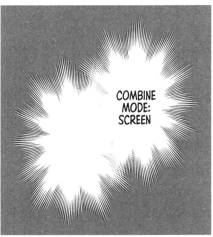

COMBINE
MODE:
SCREEN

MIURA: When layering sea urchin flashes on top of each other, place them on the same layer, go into "Combine Mode," and pick either "Relative (Brightness)" or "Screen." That way, the white part of the lower flash design will be transparent.

KOSEI: If you don't mind, could I ask a few more technical questions?

SAITO: I also have questions I've received from others.

MIURA: Of course, go ahead!

■ Can I use analog pen settings with Clip Studio Paint?

KOSEI: In CSP, are there pen settings that come out looking more like analog pens?

MIURA: CSP has a wealth of settings that are a breeze to make use of. Do a quick internet search and you'll come up with tons. Once you've got a decent handle of the program's functions, you can even create your own custom pen to suit your tastes.

■ How thick should the panel borders be, and what pen should I use?

KOSEI: Can you tell me about drawing panel borders? Which pen should I be using, and how thick should those borders be?

MIURA: Rather than drawing panel borders by hand, the paneling function is much easier to use, and it creates clean results that are easily modified on the fly. Those settings even let you adjust the border thickness at any point, and you can set it so that your art won't stick out beyond the borders. Personally, I set the border thickness to 0.5 mm. Most authors choose somewhere between 0.5 mm and 1 mm. Also, it can be a pain to break each individual page into panels over and over, so I tend to implement the standard page layout across all pages, right from the start.

SAITO: I've heard that panel borders appear thinner than they actually are, due to screen brightness, and will wind up appearing thicker than expected once printed on paper.

MIURA: That applies to the gutters between panels as well. You'll get an accurate impression of how thick those should be by blowing up existing printed manga to B4 size and measuring for yourself with a ruler.

How do I make the underdrawing fainter when doing the inking?

SAITO: How should one go about making the underdrawing fainter when doing the inking?

MIURA: Lowering a layer's opacity makes it appear fainter. You can also change the underdrawing's base color from, say, black to light blue, by selecting "Change Layer Color" from the layer palette. The default happens to be that specific light blue, but you can choose any color you wish. One warning: be careful not to make your underdrawing so faint that you forget it's still there. I've done that before, which resulted in the underdrawing being printed as part of the final product.

KOSEI: Yikes...

MIURA: Prevent that mistake by using the designated underdrawing layer function. That way, even if you forget to remove the underdrawing layer, the program stops it from being printed.

KOSEI: Oh, that's neat!

For an easier time, which layer should be on top—the underdrawing or the line drawing?

MIURA: Personally, I prefer to have the underdrawing layer on top of the line drawing layer.

KOSEI: Wait, why's that?

MIURA: With analog art, you'll add your inks on top of the pencil underdrawing, because at the end you can just erase the pencil.

KOSEI: Right, and...?

MIURA: But with digital art, removing the underdrawing is as simple as not displaying that layer, so there's no manual erasing involved. Plus, with the underdrawing layer on top (albeit fainter), you can always refer back to the underdrawing as you're adding your inks. It can even be there to provide guidelines when you're finishing up with blacks and tones.

■ In Clip Studio Paint, is there a way to only delete the tips of lines that stick out?

KOSEI: Seems like that's a huge advantage of the digital method, since erasing by hand is a real pain... By the way, when I'm doing analog art, I find that the tips of my lines often stick out past where they should, but is there a way to delete those little excess bits in CSP?

MIURA: You're looking for the "Vector Eraser" tool, which erases up to a given intersection of lines. Vectors in general are tremendously useful! You can alter the thickness of a line after drawing it, change a line to a dotted line, make a line curve, and perform all sorts of after-the-fact edits. Shrinking and enlarging won't even harm your line work. That's why I draw all my characters using vectors.

■ How do I only apply tone in an area of my choosing?

SAITO: Is there a way to only apply tone in a specified area? Say, a character's hair?

MIURA: More than doable, just by selecting the area you're interested in. Use the automatic selection tool and click on the inside of the shape to fill with tone, right up to the edges. That tone can be added from either the material palette or the selection launcher. In the event the tone doesn't fill in every spot you want (or ends up somewhere you don't want), use a pen tool (or eraser) to touch it up. I work with preset layers for my manga art, which includes layers for 10%, 20%, 30%, 40%, and 50% tone. When I use a pen or fill tool on those layers, it automatically comes out as the proper tone.

KOSEI: Oh, smart thinking!

MIURA: In addition, to make it easier to distinguish the different density levels, I display each tone level in a different color. However, for the back half of *Yuuna and the Haunted Hot Springs*, I started drawing my drafts in gray, so the tone functions weren't available to me. Instead of taking advantage of the tone display options, I just employed different layer colors to better see what I was working with.

SAITO: Is there a way to adjust a tone's density once it's already on the canvas?

MIURA: Go to the "Layer Property" palette (accessed via the "Window" menu at the top of the screen), and then find "Density" in "Tone Settings."

How do I create a perspective drawing?

KOSEI: I struggle a lot with perspective drawings when working with physical pen and paper. Are the ruler tools in CSP useful for that sort of thing?

MIURA: Yes, CSP's perspective ruler allows you to place the vanishing point at a location outside the canvas, whereas achieving the same thing in analog would involve tacking on an extra piece of paper to your draft paper. You can even create perspective rulers to accommodate 3D shapes and spaces. I like the 3D stuff for my backgrounds, so I don't really use the perspective ruler to draw buildings, but rather to add a touch of perspective to 3D lines.

When do I use the eraser tool, versus a white pen?

SAITO: Can you explain the difference between the eraser tool and a pen set to white?

MIURA: I don't think many artists would ever use a white pen for the purpose of erasing lines drawn on a layer, though many might opt for a transparent pen effect. As for eraser versus transparent pen on a raster layer? No notable difference. The only real use for a white pen would be hiding the layers underneath. There's more of a difference with these things when you start using the vector layers I mentioned before.

KOSEI: Hmm... This is all getting a little complicated for a novice like me to keep up with!

SAITO: There's no sense in trying to memorize all these details now. You'll start to remember as you encounter each function in practice, since necessity is the mother of true learning.

MIURA: Exactly. I should also mention that the eraser tool also comes with a vector eraser function. You can't replicate that when using the transparency pen. That vector eraser lets you erase up to the intersection, or the entire line, which comes in handy. Trying it out for yourself is more informative than any explanation, though.

SAITO: What's the difference between those last two things you mentioned?

MIURA: Erasing up to the intersection will only erase the little tip of a line that hangs over another line, whereas the whole line option will delete the entirety of a single line, even if it's in the middle of a dense cluster of lines.

KOSEI: I could make use of that for sure!

MIURA: The eraser tool also comes with the "Erase All Layers" function, which, with a single stroke, will apply the eraser effect to every layer at once, whether working with vector layers or raster layers. That's another thing you can't replicate with a transparent pen.

■ What Do I look out for when exporting data?

SAITO: Newer authors with some experience drawing for publications and amateurs who've done *dojinshi* work often wonder what to look out for when exporting their digital data. According to one new author, "The number one easy-to-make mistake is exporting grayscale art and having the line drawing converted to tones when it prints in the magazine."

MIURA: That problem is less about exporting data and more about layer settings. If you don't want the edges of your lines being converted to tones, then use a monochrome layer instead of a grayscale one. Go into the "Layer Property" palette, find "Expression Color," and switch from "Gray" to "Monochrome." As long as you don't choose "Apply Expression Color of Preview," then what's displayed and what's printed will be monochrome, while your gray data is still preserved.

SAITO: Good to know. I'll pass along that info.

■ How do I adjust the size of my draft for exporting?

MIURA: When you're shrinking your art for export, go to "Export Settings," then "Advanced Settings of Color," then "Export Settings for Tone," "Frequency," and select "Depend on Export Scale." Also be sure to click the box for "Enable Tone Effect for Layer." Failure to do so will alter how tones are displayed or even export them as grays.

KOSEI: How terrifying...

MIURA: It's fine to submit grayscale files for volume releases, but publication in *Jump* magazines demands monochrome (duotone) files.

KOSEI: Sure, of course. I'll keep that detail in mind.

MIURA: Meaning, if you've drawn your art in grayscale but need to export it for *Jump*, then go to "Export Settings," "Color," "Expression Color," and pick "Duotone (Toning)." That will export all your grays as halftone dots of varying densities. That all-important frequency setting can be found as "Default Frequency" in the "Canvas" section of the "New" dialog box. Once your new project is created, you can go back and adjust that default frequency at any time via "Canvas Properties" under "Edit."

SAITO: Thank you so much for the information. I think we've both learned a lot.

MIURA: Keep in mind that your export settings will depend on your own preferences, so one size doesn't fit all.

KOSEI: Thanks a lot for explaining everything so well! I'm gonna work hard to get to the point where I actually gotta think about prepping digital files for publication in *Jump*!

SAITO: In addition to Clip Studio Paint, there's also *Jump*'s official, completely free program for creating manga called "Jump Paint by Medibang"! Give that a try as well!

CHAPTER 5 KEY POINTS

- For those unfamiliar with digital art, a pen display may be easier to work with than a pen tablet, since it feels more like working with pen and paper.

- When choosing which device to purchase, go for one that's at least a few years old, with a lot of positive user reviews.

- Back up your data with an online storage service like Dropbox just in case.

- Clip Studio Paint has a "Shueisha manga A" preset that should give you the correct canvas size (equivalent to standard draft paper).

- The digital approach can be tremendously useful once you've got a handle on drawing, but there's a lot to learn all at once. Just get started and learn as you go.

FREQUENTLY ASKED QUESTIONS FROM NEW AUTHORS

PART 3

Q 3
I'm worried that people will say I'm plagiarizing manga stories that already exist.

A
First of all, which aspect is the possibly problematic one? The art? The world? Character designs and personalities? The dialogue?

If it's the art, then try borrowing gag faces from one series but the coloring style from another (for instance). If it's the world, then change up either the time period or the physical location. If it's the characters (who resemble preexisting characters in gender, strengths, shortcomings, appearance, etc.) then add your own spin, remove other elements, or change up their age or gender. If it's the dialogue, then take influence from a wider variety of media.

You're most likely concerned about accusations of plagiarism because you're drawing from too few influences. Diversify your sources of inspiration to lend your own work more originality.

CHAPTER 6

CHOOSING THE RIGHT TOOLS

A TALK WITH KEITARO YOTSUYA SENSEI AND YUMIYA TASHIRO SENSEI!

The number of authors choosing to make manga digitally may be on the rise, but there's still something special about the good old analog methods! In either case, what really matters is finding the approach that suits you best! In this chapter, a pair of professionals will discuss how to choose the right analog tools for you, based on their own experiences!

THE PROS

Keitaro Yotsuya
Author of *Akuma no Memu Memu-chan*, which runs on Jump+. Has an established reputation—even among other pros—for his clean, readable work.

Yumiya Tashiro
Author of *Black Clover Gaiden: Quartet Knights* (six volumes total). He's worked in any number of analog manga studios, either as the primary author or as an assistant.

■ Tell us the steps and amount of time that go into making a draft.

YOTSUYA: First off, for *Memu Memu-chan*, I do everything up through the line art the analog way, and then I switch to digital for finishing. Sometimes I do corrections and touch-ups on paper, but most of the time it's digital at that point.

On *Memu Memu-chan*, I'll do my underdrawing on plain old printer paper, then use a copy machine (household model) to copy it onto proper draft paper, in blue, before adding inks. This eliminates the need for erasers for the most part and affects what sort of tools I'm choosing. If your underdrawing ends up needing lots of corrections, the paper can get kind of beaten-up, which results in the ink bleeding later on. With my method, that isn't a concern at all.

I never worked as an assistant, so I had to research the more popular tools on the internet. I tried out a wide variety before settling on the ones that worked best for me.

In terms of labor hours, I draw for about ten hours per day, which produces three and a half pages on a good day (that's just inking the characters, though). Compared to the authors with weekly series, I'm horribly slow. My priority at this point isn't speed, but level of polish, which also affects which tools I choose.

Note that I can only speak from my own experience. Every author will have their own pen pressure and bring their own habits (good or bad) to the table, so I recommend trying out a number of tools and methods.

TASHIRO: Assuming I'm in peak condition and on top of my game, I can finish five pages in a ten-hour day. Maybe three pages on a more average day. I've been finishing off with digital lately, but my past series were done in full analog from start to finish.

Fun fact—back in my early days, once I was done with my assistant work for the day, I would spend another two to four hours just sitting there drawing lines. More fun than you might think. When starting out, it's pretty crucial to focus on upping your capacity, but the best practice for me was giving it my all as an assistant in a pro's studio! Being surrounded by talented folks is an amazing way to boost your own skills.

Now that the shoe's on the other foot and I have my own studio, I notice that the newbie assistants improve by leaps and bounds when they can glance over at the work the senior assistants are doing and take inspiration. Getting to witness a proper manga draft come into being is the ultimate way to study and learn. In my case, I would take cell phone pics of the great art I'd see in the studio, and file it away in folders on my phone. After work, I'd go home, stare at one of those fantastic drawings (of, say, a chair) from my senior colleagues, and try reproducing them by hand. Copying an amazing chair might be all you need to suddenly add "amazing chair" to your repertoire. In short, **witness great art in the making, and then copy it**.

■ What are the key points when choosing the right set of art tools?

UNDERDRAWING PEN
(mechanical pencil, standard pencil)

4B Mechanical Pencil

YOTSUYA: I use **Ain Stein** refills (from **Pentel**). For whatever reason, those pencil lines erase really cleanly. There's probably not a huge difference between brands, but some mechanical pencil refills seem to snap easily, or just don't work well in other ways, so try out several options.

3B Pencil

YOTSUYA: The pencils made by **Staedtler** (from **Staedtler Japan**) may be pricey, but I'm a die-hard fan because of just how sharp they get when sharpened. I prefer a darker, deeper graphite because I make those blue copies of my underdrawings before inking, which eliminates the need for erasing. I also don't tend to press down very hard, but these pencils produce intense lines nonetheless. If you plan to do a bunch of erasing after your inks are down, I recommend a 2B pencil.

Pencil graphite hardness is ranked as follows (from hardest to softest): 9H to H ➡ F ➡ HB ➡ B to 6B. The closer you get to 9H, the harder the graphite and the fainter the lines you're drawing, while the side closer to 6B has softer graphite and produces darker lines. The harder graphite tends to damage your paper more, while the softer stuff is harder to erase (because it comes out darker). The most common grades used for manga are B or 2B.

I actually used to use blue refills for my mechanical pencils, because the graphite is soft and easy to draw with, and I had no reason to do any erasing. The downside was that my lines would end up extra thick when I added inks, so I abandoned that approach. There are a number of factors that affect how thick the lines turn out, but for whatever reason, using the blue pencil and then ink on **I-C** draft paper (from **G-Too**) resulted in particularly thick lines, whereas regular black graphite didn't make the lines any thicker. Note that the problem of the thicker lines after using blue pencil is remedied if you do your inking with a fineliner.

I've also found that using blue mechanical pencil for the underdrawing and then a nib for inks (on **Art Color** draft paper, from **Namura Taiseido**) results in the ink bleeding like crazy. In short, line thickness and the bleeding factor when inking are affected by several things, like your paper, your ink, your nib, and your underdrawing lines. So, it may have nothing to do with your skill level. It's important to experiment by changing up your paper, your ink, or whatever.

TASHIRO: I use regular B mechanical pencils for my underdrawings. My debut manga was done with blue pencil, but that can leave your paper a total mess. I like to be able to envision what my inks will look like at the underdrawing stage, so I prefer darker pencil lines. Throughout my career, I've always done my storyboards the analog way.

PEN FOR DRAWING CHARACTERS
(G-pen, mapping nib, etc.)

YOTSUYA: Pens are categorized depending on what sort of lines they're good for—thick, standard, or thin.

○ **THICK LINES**

Brush Pen (**Bimoji**: extra fine or fine, from **Kuretake**)

YOTSUYA: Using a regular G-pen for close-ups of your characters will result in lines that are too thin. Traditional brushes are hard to control, so I opt for a softer felt-tip pen (either firm nib or soft nib).

While working on *Memu Memu-chan*, I wanted thicker lines, so I marched over to the stationery store and bought up every type of brush pen they had. Turns out, the Bimoji one suited my needs best. I also loved how it felt to draw with the **Fudemakase** (from **Pilot Corporation**) and the **Fudegokochi** (from **Kuretake**), but both of them had big problems with bleeding when I went to apply Misnon correction fluid. I didn't bother trying other brands of correction fluid, since I already liked the Bimoji pen well enough. I rejected the other options I tested out for having ink that was too thin, brush tips that were too soft, or what have you. On the other hand, a brand-new extra fine Bimoji has a thin tip that allows for lines of varying intensity, just like a G-pen.

Felt-Tip Pen (thick, from **Mitsubishi Pencil**)

YOTSUYA: This is what I use for extreme close-ups of Memu Memu. It allows for uniformly thick lines, which lends her a sort of goofy cuteness.

○ **STANDARD LINES**

Fineliner (**Pigma**: 0.3 mm, 0.1 mm, from **Sakura Cray-Pas**)

YOTSUYA: I use the 0.3 mm or 0.1 mm fineliner for midrange shots of characters (as opposed to close-ups). I still lean on the thicker side for those lines, since the characters tend to fade into the background if the lines are too thin. *Memu Memu-chan* is supposed to look cutesy, so I prefer a fineliner without much range of thickness. More specifically, I use the one from Pigma, which has this nice, dark ink. Plus, it feels great in the hand, so it's just a nice pen for general use.

I haven't tested out many of the types of fineliners out there, but you'll find that different brands offer inks of varying darkness and nibs of differing hardness and shape. I don't tend to hold my pen upright, so I have trouble drawing lines properly when the nib juts out only a little. Pens like that aren't for me. Nor do I use the kind that can be partially erased by an eraser.

G-Pen (**Zebra Chrome G-Pen**, from **Zebra**)

YOTSUYA: G-pens were my primary tool for most of *Memu Memu-chan*, and Zebra might be the most famous brand. I like how their nibs are nice and pointed but also flexible enough to really open up. With a fineliner, you have to layer lines on top of each other to adjust the boldness, but with a G-pen, you have that control with every single line. That's really handy, since it lets you draw faster.

When it comes to pen nibs, I have three categories: brand-new ones, ones I've used for a bit, and ones I've been using forever. The tips of the older ones get rounded off and become even more flexible, which is great for drawing thicker lines. These days, though, using a G-pen tires out my arm, so it's no longer my tool of choice. On the other hand, fineliners lend a cutesy look to the art, which is a perfect fit for Memu Memu-chan. For many years I thought that mastering nib pens was a worthwhile challenge because they help improve the art, but at some point I started to suspect that G-pens are better suited to artists who are already fantastic at what they do and are just trying to up their speed. What's the truth? Who knows? I do think G-pens let you draw faster than fineliners, at least once you've mastered them.

As for the penholder, try a bunch until you find the one that's right for you. Maybe you're someone who prefers to wrap a bunch of tape around it, giving you something nice and thick to grip. That method probably prevents the hand from getting worn out too quickly. They say Akira Toriyama Sensei likes to chop off the back end and wield a much shorter pen, but when I tried that, I found myself unable to draw long, graceful strokes. **Everyone holds a pen and manipulates it in their own way**, so you ought to test out different approaches. The fineliner penholder is basically my ideal, in terms of thickness and length.

○ **THIN LINES**

Fineliner (**Pigma**: 0.05 mm, 0.03 mm, from **Sakura Cray-Pas**)

YOTSUYA: This is what I use when drawing tiny characters at a distance. The 0.03 mm one is really thin, so it's only for special occasions.

Mapping nib (**Zebra** Mapping Pen A, from **Zebra**)

YOTSUYA: Only for the finest of details, like midrange shots of a character's eyes. Thick outlines are useful to keep a character from fading into the background, but if every line of the character is thick, then there's too much black and the details are lost. So those inner lines should be thinner than the outlines.

Truly talented artists can imply different textures with their lines, but I've pretty much only got the two options—thick outlines and thin inner lines. I'm always impressed when a pro can use different lines for hair, clothing, male skin, female skin, and so on.

TASHIRO: For thin lines, I take the orthodox route and mostly stick to G-pens. Thin wrinkles might warrant a fineliner, but generally, I keep two types of G-pens on hand.

Type A: a newer pen, for finer lines

Type B: an older pen, better for thick lines because of its splayed tip

I mostly draw my characters with Type B, and then I go over some of the lines with Type A for emphasis. By the time my current Type B is ready to be thrown out, usually a Type A is ready to graduate to a Type B. Then I'll open up a new pen nib, giving birth to a Type A (sorry if that's confusing).

When practicing with an unfamiliar pen, I recommend writing なにぬねの [na-ni-nu-ne-no, in Japanese hiragana characters] over and over. Those shapes are a great way to get used to a particular pen. I think all the curves in there help me get past the stage when a brand-new pen feels stiff and tricky to use. Also, find a ruler and practice drawing straight lines that taper either at the start or the end. Basic line-drawing practice. Your mastery over where the line tapers (and where it doesn't) is a big factor in getting better at art in general.

Another tool I recommend is the **Futayaku Double-Sided Brush Pen** (from **Pilot**). Please use this divine gift from the heavens! [*laughs*] It's got a thick side and a thin side, making it at least 100 percent more capable than most other pens. Get good enough with it, and you'll be drawing lots of your primary lines with the thin side. I suggest using the thin side for outlines and the thick side for filling in your blacks. What usually stands out to me about a new artist's swaths of black isn't that they do it poorly, but that they aren't using the right tools. **Mackee** (from **Zebra**) is another good option. That sort of work shouldn't be done with big splashy strokes, but rather by squashing your brush against the paper. The splashy strokes will often result in leakage, so instead, think of it as slowly pressing the ink down to fill in a wide area. That's my take.

PEN FOR DRAWING THINGS BESIDES CHARACTERS
(fineliner, brush pen)

○ **BORDERS**

Fineliner (**Pigma**: 0.8 mm, from **Sakura Cray-Pas**)

YOTSUYA: I once read in some interview that many *Jump* authors prefer the 0.8 mm fineliner, so that's what I went with. Now and then I draw borders digitally, but most of the time I do my lines analog and scan them in. This is because I feel that digitally drawn borders inevitably have a colder, inorganic look to them.

○ **WORD BALLOONS**

Brush Pen (**Bimoji**: extra fine, fine, from **Kuretake**)

YOTSUYA: Word balloons should stand out just as much as the characters themselves, so I draw them with thick lines. That said, some authors use thinner lines. You just don't want the word balloons fading into the backgrounds.

○ **BACKGROUNDS**

Fineliner (**Pigma**: 0.1 mm, 0.05 mm, from **Sakura Cray-Pas**)

YOTSUYA: On the other hand, backgrounds should not stand out more than the characters, so I prefer thinner lines. Too thin, though, and they lose all semblance of cuteness. Lately, my assistants have been doing backgrounds digitally.

TASHIRO: I use a 0.8 mm fineliner for my borders. Other details get either a 0.1 mm or 0.03 mm pen, but those become extremely faint when I apply an eraser. There's a pretty limited use for those.

INK

Lettering Sol (from **Kaimei**)

YOTSUYA: Seriously dark ink. Impervious to damage from erasers. I used to use **Document Ink** (from **Pilot**), but those lines would fade a little when I went over them with an eraser. Still, that brand produces high-quality ink that makes for lovely lines, and there are plenty of artists who use Pilot's Drafting Pen Ink or Document Ink. The **Kaimei Bokujyu** ink from **Kaimei** also yields nice-looking lines, but it takes longer to dry.

Drafting Pen Ink (from **Pilot**)

TASHIRO: Pretty sure that's what most people use.

DRAFT PAPER

Art Color draft paper (from **Namura Taiseido**)

YOTSUYA: Nib pens often end up catching on this paper, and the way it makes ink bleed causes me lots of stress, but it sucks up ink in just the right way to produce nice lines with a fineliner. I used **I-C draft paper** (from **G-Too**) for many years, but it's almost too slick... The way it repels ink made it hard for me to create pleasing lines. Fineliners, in particular, slip and slide right across the surface, resulting in lines that are too faint. Not a good fit for me.

I started out drawing the characters of *Memu Memu-chan* with a G-pen, but I found that work exhausting, so I switched to fineliners (and a new type of paper). Still, if we're to believe the internet, more people use that I-C paper than any other type. It wasn't right for me, but obviously lots of people think it's worthy.

Each brand's draft paper is going to receive ink differently, or make certain pens catch, or make others bleed, so I suggest buying a range of types to test out. Once upon a time, I was working on a one-shot and I bought a particular brand's paper because the package design looked cool. I did thirty-one whole pages of underdrawings, but to my dismay, when I went to add the inks, the ink bled everywhere. I was so demotivated that I never even finished that one...

Another point to consider—when draft paper is exposed to humidity, your ink will bleed terribly, so be careful how you store your paper. That's one reason that I do my inks immediately after the underdrawing is done.

And if your characters' faces aren't drawn well in your underdrawing—necessitating lots of corrections and erasing—the paper can get damaged, which also leads to bleeding ink. One strategy there is to use a light box and trace onto an entirely new sheet of paper.

TASHIRO: I have a heavy hand, so I prefer **I-C draft paper** (from **G-Too**). If you have a lighter touch, your strokes will bounce right off the I-C paper, in which case I recommend **Deleter** comic paper (from **Deleter**). There's a popular conception that shojo manga authors prefer Deleter-brand paper.

ERASER

MONO eraser and kneaded eraser (from Tonbo Enpitsu)

YOTSUYA: I use the standard size for most erasing and the jumbo size when I need to erase large swathes. I hate the especially sticky kneaded erasers, so I avoid them. Their ability to morph into different shapes is useful for pinpoint erasing, but some brands can leave behind little eraser shavings, so watch out for that. I've tried electric erasers before, but they produce lots of chunky shavings. Not my cup of tea. Also, kneaded erasers are great for cleaning off stray bits of screentone.

TASHIRO: I like kneaded erasers made for working with tone. I use three types of erasers, and one of them is for general use with draft paper. I also recommend the pen-style eraser **MONO zero** (from **Tonbo Enpitsu**)! It's awesome. Very handy for erasing delicate lines. Normal erasers will often wipe out more than you want, but the pen-type eraser makes it feel like you're precisely wielding an actual pen.

CORRECTION FLUID

Misnon (from Lion Jimuki)

YOTSUYA: I use both Misnon as is and Misnon that's been watered down (with actual water). With the latter, I'll dip my nib pen right into it and basically draw white lines. The water-to-Misnon ratio can be tricky to figure out, so I start with a cup already containing water and add Misnon until it's just right.

TASHIRO: Misnon (from **Lion Jimuki**) is just right for covering up big areas. Not so easy for smaller, delicate spots... Those demand something like **Dr. Ph. Martin's** brand. That's better when you want to dunk your pen in the fluid itself. Correction fluid comes in those two types, basically.

■ What tools do I need besides the basics like pens and erasers?

LIGHT BOX

MUTOH Tracer Light Board (B4) (from Mutoh Industries)

YOTSUYA: Nice and thin, and you can adjust the level of light.

TASHIRO: There are two types of light boxes—the touch type and the slide type. With the touch type, you press your finger down for two or three seconds to turn the light on or off. But my assistants are constantly flicking the light on and off, so they prefer the slide type.

RULER

YOTSUYA: I'm not too familiar with rulers, since I don't do my saturated lines in analog, but I think the best ones are transparent, with grid patterns. Ink can smudge onto rulers, so be sure to clean them off frequently.

FRENCH CURVE

YOTSUYA: This tool is good for curved saturated action lines and special effect lines. I know the basics of how to use one, but I generally don't bother, so I won't even attempt to explain. I'm betting young people these days aren't too familiar with the French curve.

TASHIRO: I don't use this. Too tricky.

STENCIL

YOTSUYA: This would be a thin plastic sheet with a number of perfect circles and ovals cut out of it—perfect for creating clean word balloons, which is exactly what some authors use it for. I'm not one of those authors, but it's certainly useful if you're doing your finishing touches in analog.

TASHIRO: I'm a huge fan of **Template W-2** (from **Banko**)! I don't have many opportunities to implement those circles that the stencil provides (I find it hard to use that way), but I do use the stencil somewhat like a compass, to achieve curves at specific angles. Having that plastic edge keeps the ink from bleeding. I actually have a veteran assistant who swears by stencils and carries around this compact one that folds in half. I'm a fan of that one. Definitely indispensable if you're trying to draw complex curves by hand for your backgrounds, so I buy them for my assistants, and I recommend them for authors who work in full analog.

UTILITY KNIFE

TASHIRO: I use a regular utility knife and a design knife. The latter is good for cutting through tone and making delicate moves (it's easily chipped and blunted, though). For fine-tuning, I use the side of a regular utility knife.

TAPE

YOTSUYA: I like **mending tape**, which is clear, and which doesn't leave sticky residue when peeled away. When drawing saturated lines, I'll secure a piece of that tape to the center point with a thumbtack.

TRACING PAPER

YOTSUYA: When inserting inner monologue dialogue (floating text without word balloons), I'll stick tracing paper, which is nearly transparent, on top of my draft paper and do the lettering in pencil.

SCREENTONE

TASHIRO: It's hard to recommend a certain brand since the products I've used keep getting discontinued. Even authors who work largely in analog have in recent times switched to digital if only for tones and blacks, including me. I draw my characters in analog before switching to digital for tones.

☆ When your art isn't emerging the way you'd like, the issue may not be solely a matter of skill. It may be that you're using the wrong tools.

Everyone holds a pen differently and applies a certain amount of pressure to the page, so don't go assuming that the famous name brand tools are necessarily best for you. Try out a variety.

FREQUENTLY ASKED QUESTIONS FROM NEW AUTHORS

PART 4

Q 4
I'm having doubts about how interesting my creation is, and I've ground to a halt. I'm thinking I just suck at this...

A
Those doubts are inevitable. But those doubts will multiply even more when you brood about your lack of progress. Finishing projects is the only way to move forward, so keep working, finish your stuff, and get it evaluated. Believing that you suck is a matter of setting the bar too high and having lofty ideals for your work. That's not a height you can reach in a single leap. **Gradual, step-by-step growth comes from finishing projects. All your toil and labor contribute to your drawing hand's muscle memory. Finish the work, and the growth is sure to follow.**

Q5

They often say that authors should imbue their work with their own painful experiences and emotional damage, but do I have to involve that painful stuff in what I'm creating?

A

Are those painful experiences something you want to draw? Something that you simply have to put down on the page? If not, then forget about it. **Nothing good can come from content you have to force yourself to create.** Naturally there's some subject matter an author would rather not touch on at all.

Q6

I just came up with a great new idea while in the middle of a project. Should I drop every-thing and switch to that new idea?

A

Finish what you're already working on first. No matter how great that new idea is, the top priority should be finishing current projects. The people who can see things through are the ones who dominate this and other creative industries. **Just start on that new thing after finishing your current piece. That idea's not going anywhere.**

Q 7

I submitted for a manga prize but didn't even make it as a finalist. Am I just not cut out for manga?

A

More than likely, your submission was lacking on its own merits. Don't view your not winning a contest as a complete rejection of you as a creator. There are examples of authors who created years' worth of manga that refused to bear fruit, but who immediately won a prize when they switched gears and tried out a new style of story. It's impossible to predict exactly how a given author will grow and improve, so we recommend trying something new and different, and/or bringing your work to an editor in the hope of discovering what your greatest assets are and what you're suited to.

Q 8

How strictly do I have to follow the rules and advice given in this book?

A

Frankly, feel free to ignore all of this. All you'll find in the pages of this book are opinions from the *Weekly Shonen Jump* editorial staff, based on our own limited experiences. Nothing would make us happier than you making use of the advice that strikes a chord with you while ignoring the bits that don't resonate as much.

1

READ THIS WAY

BUILDING: SHUEISHA

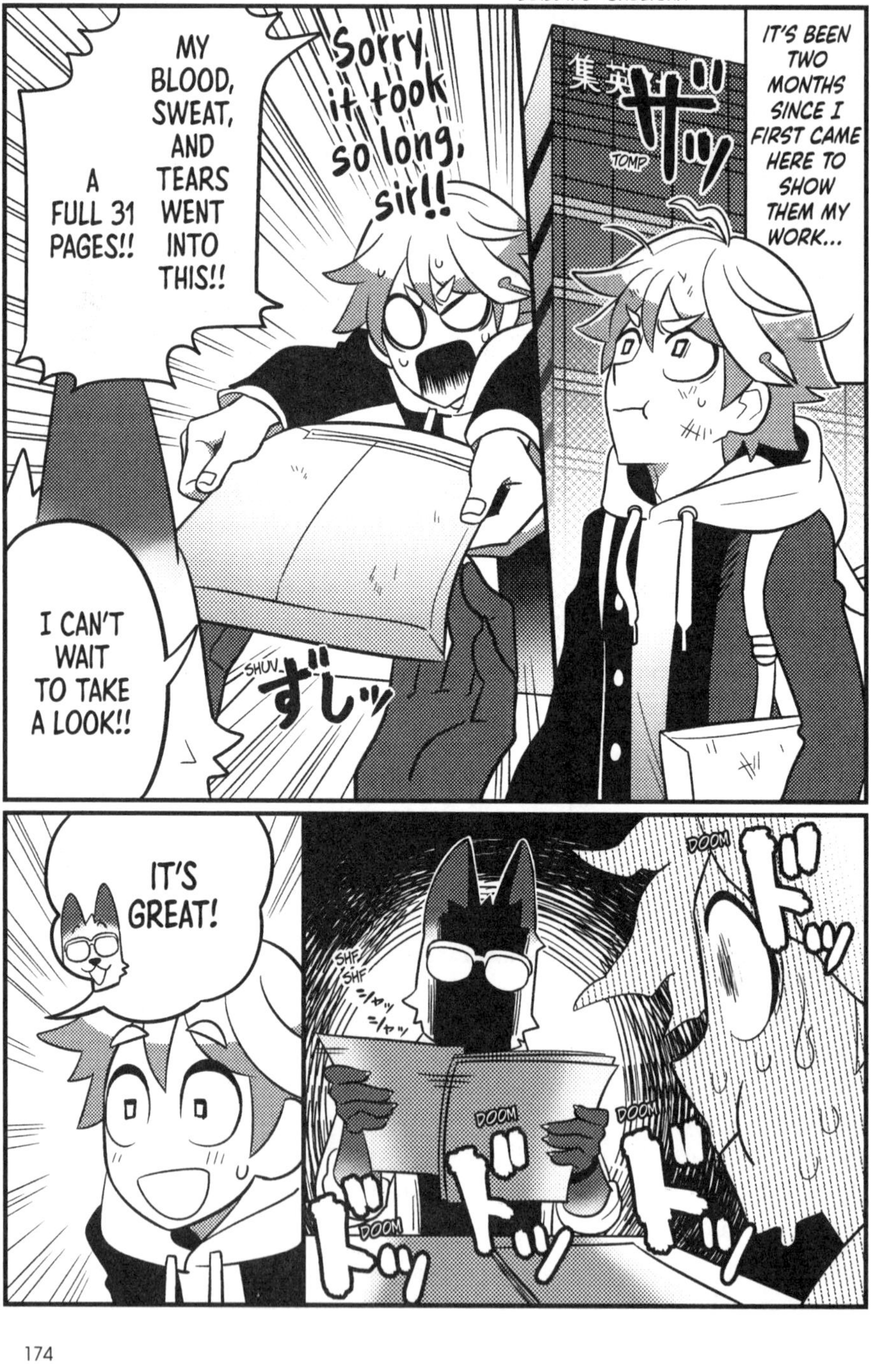

IT'S BEEN TWO MONTHS SINCE I FIRST CAME HERE TO SHOW THEM MY WORK...
TOMP
Sorry it took so long, sir!!
MY BLOOD, SWEAT, AND TEARS WENT INTO THIS!!
A FULL 31 PAGES!!
SHUV
I CAN'T WAIT TO TAKE A LOOK!!
DOOM
SHF SHF
DOOM
DOOM
DOOM
IT'S GREAT!

8

READ THIS WAY

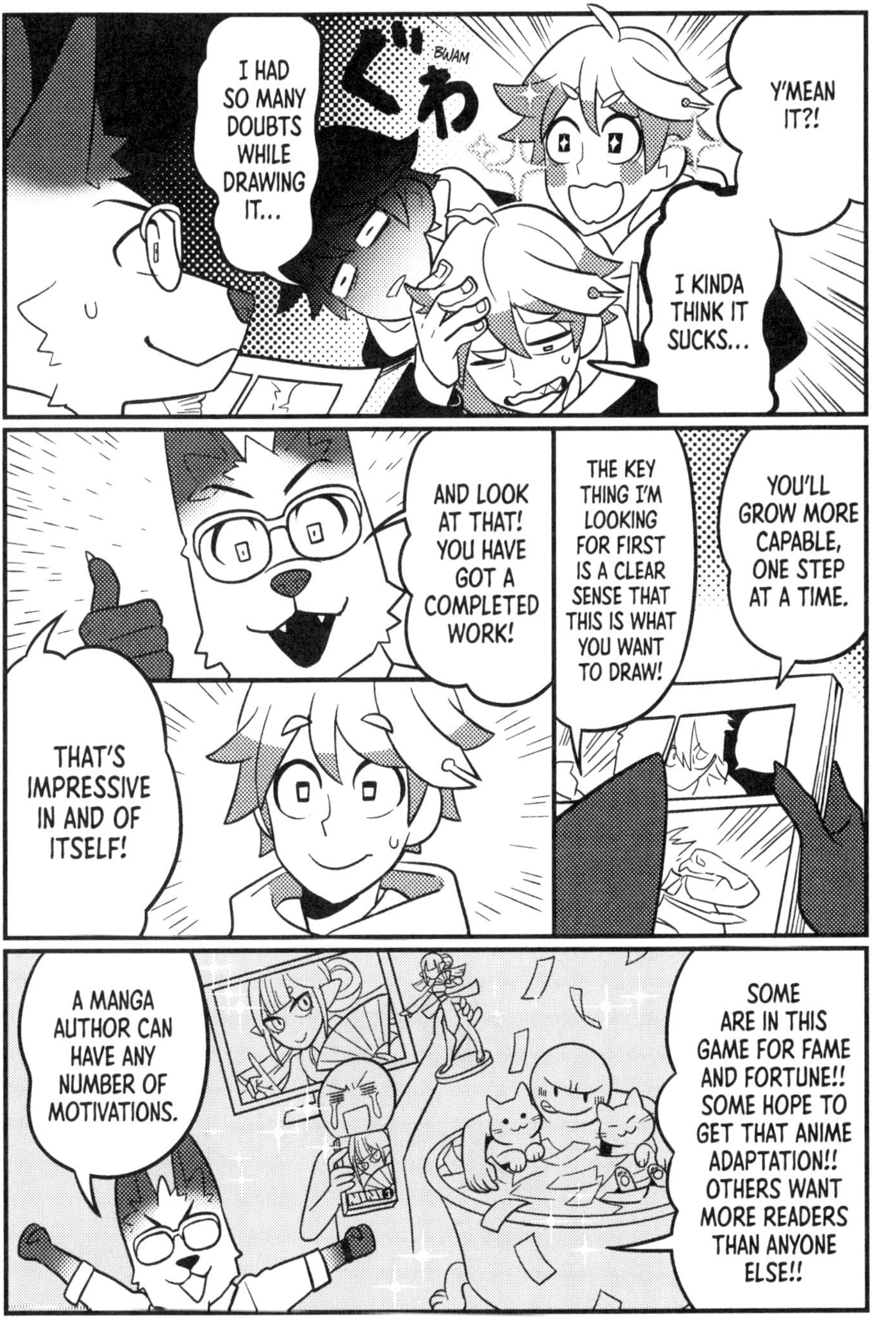

Y'MEAN IT?!
I KINDA THINK IT SUCKS...
ぐゎ
BWAM
I HAD SO MANY DOUBTS WHILE DRAWING IT...
YOU'LL GROW MORE CAPABLE, ONE STEP AT A TIME.
THE KEY THING I'M LOOKING FOR FIRST IS A CLEAR SENSE THAT THIS IS WHAT YOU WANT TO DRAW!
AND LOOK AT THAT! YOU HAVE GOT A COMPLETED WORK!
THAT'S IMPRESSIVE IN AND OF ITSELF!
SOME ARE IN THIS GAME FOR FAME AND FORTUNE!! SOME HOPE TO GET THAT ANIME ADAPTATION!! OTHERS WANT MORE READERS THAN ANYONE ELSE!!
A MANGA AUTHOR CAN HAVE ANY NUMBER OF MOTIVATIONS.

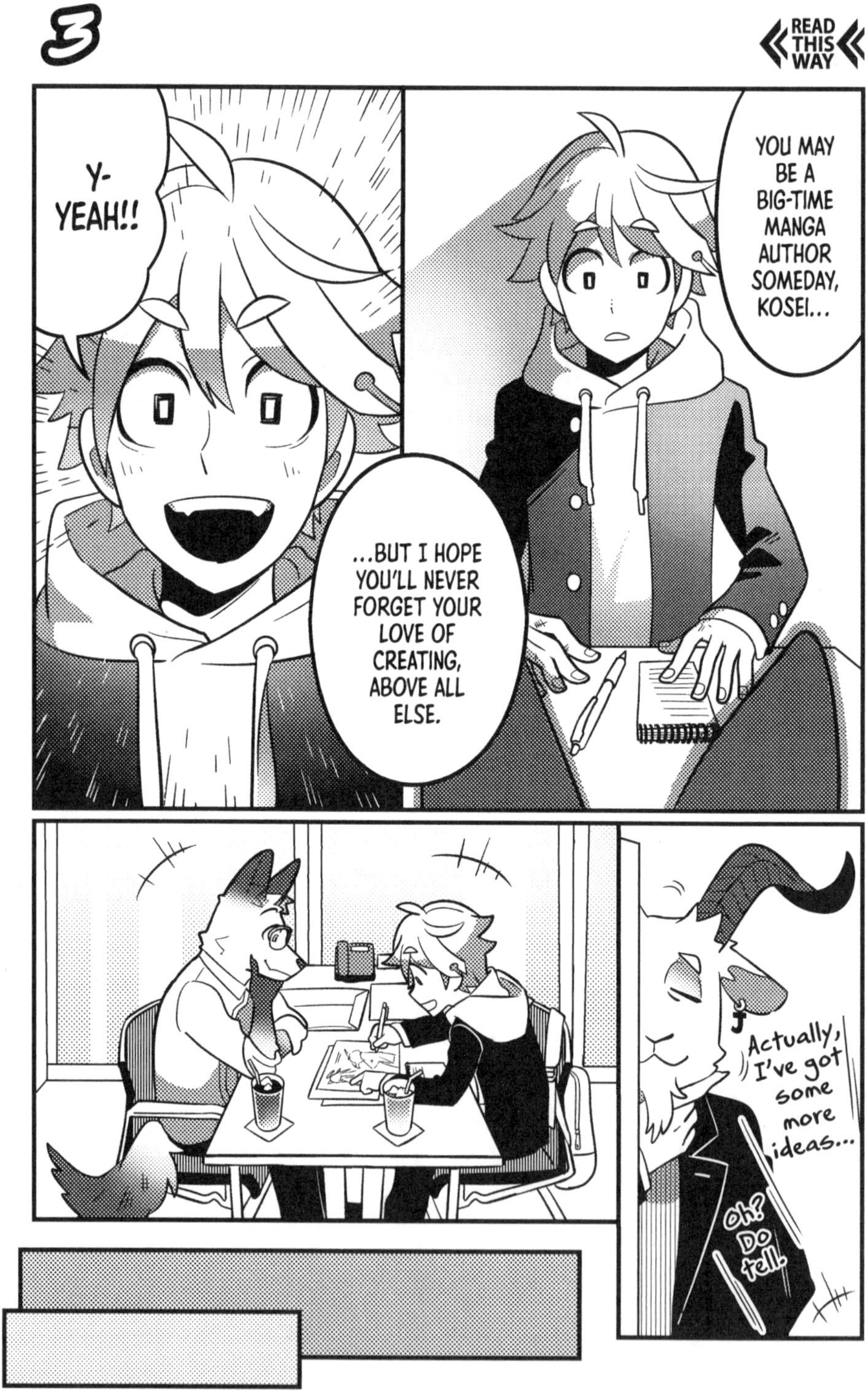
3
READ THIS WAY
YOU MAY BE A BIG-TIME MANGA AUTHOR SOMEDAY, KOSEI...
...BUT I HOPE YOU'LL NEVER FORGET YOUR LOVE OF CREATING, ABOVE ALL ELSE.
Y-YEAH!!
Actually, I've got some more ideas...
Oh? Do tell.

4

READ THIS WAY

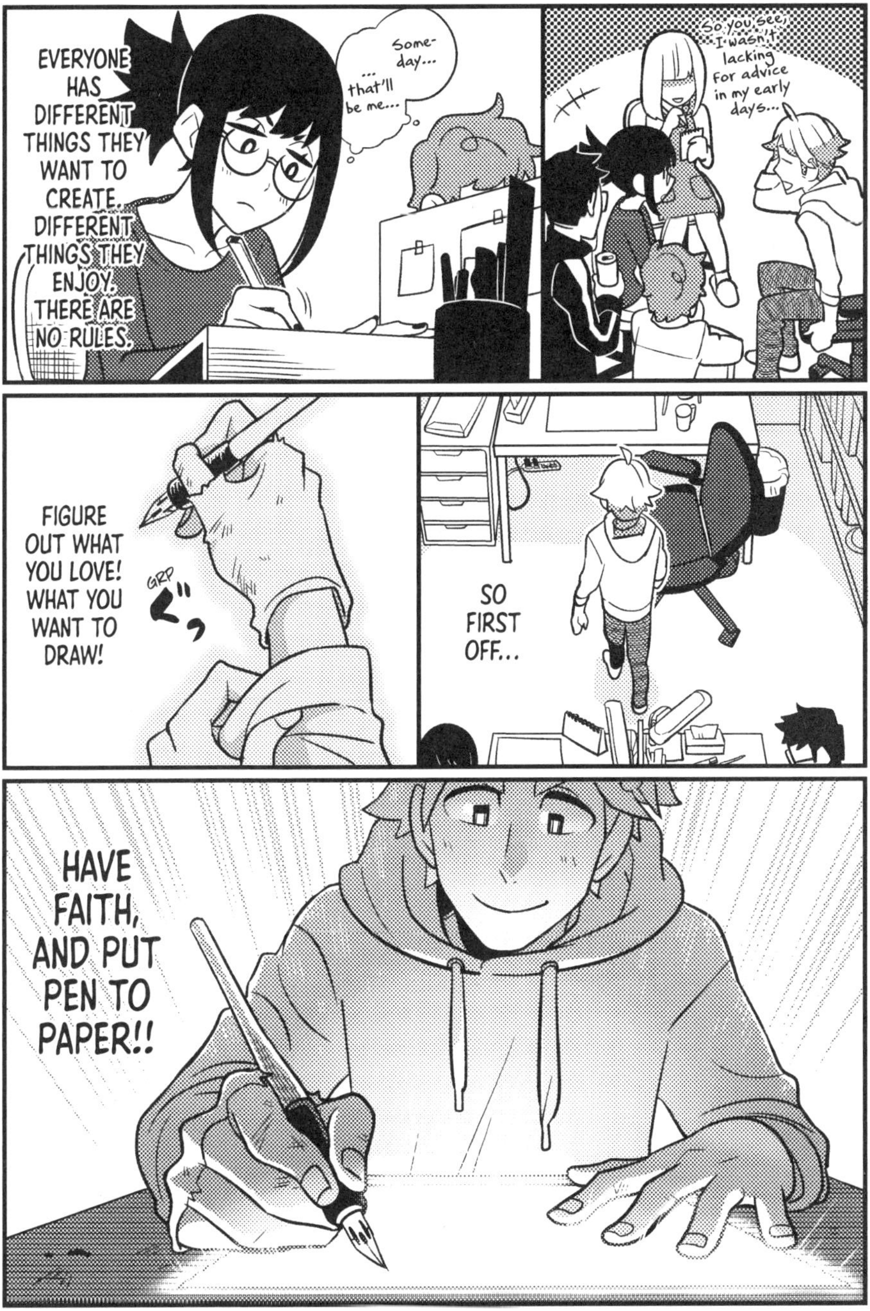

So you see, I wasn't lacking for advice in my early days...
Someday... ...that'll be me...
EVERYONE HAS DIFFERENT THINGS THEY WANT TO CREATE. DIFFERENT THINGS THEY ENJOY. THERE ARE NO RULES.
SO FIRST OFF...
FIGURE OUT WHAT YOU LOVE! WHAT YOU WANT TO DRAW!
GRP
HAVE FAITH, AND PUT PEN TO PAPER!!

IN CLOSING

This was originally conceived as a "rule book" for aspiring manga authors who've been inspired by the works found in *Weekly Shonen Jump* in recent years. However, as explained at the start, we decided to take the book in a different direction. The focus shifted to one repeated message—draw what you like—and centered more on the necessary frame of mind when considering this career.

During the process of compiling this book, we got the opportunity to read some manga created by a certain *Jump* author back during their school days. To be blunt, the art was lacking, and it wasn't clear at all what sort of story was being told—but what was abundantly clear was this author's sheer enthusiasm, which practically screamed, "This is what I wanted to create!" It's that sort of factor that makes you want to throw your support behind an author, where you can draw a clear line from the early work's personality to the author's current series.

While reading, we came to the conclusion that back then, this budding author might have been discouraged if someone had come along and given them a list of strict rules to follow when making manga. They might've thought their own style was no good, or that the medium itself was too constraining. Their distinctive style might've become homogenized, losing what made it so special. Just like that, *Jump* might have lost one of its future shining stars, and the current lineup would be all the lesser for it.

What *Jump* editors should be telling young authors isn't the secret to the cleverest way to break your page into panels or anything like that, but rather, "Don't hide what makes you yourself. Run ahead at full speed! We can teach you the tips and tricks for efficient storytelling later, but in the meantime, you'll get better by drawing, so let those ideas explode onto the paper!" Of this, we have no doubt.

That's our message to everyone, and that's how you end up with the sort of manga that our editorial department puts in *Weekly Shonen Jump*. Set that melting pot of yours to boil, believe in the strength of your ingredients, and serve it all up, piping hot, on some draft paper. Then, throw caution to the wind and follow young Kosei's lead by showing us your work or entering a manga contest. Let's make some amazing manga together!

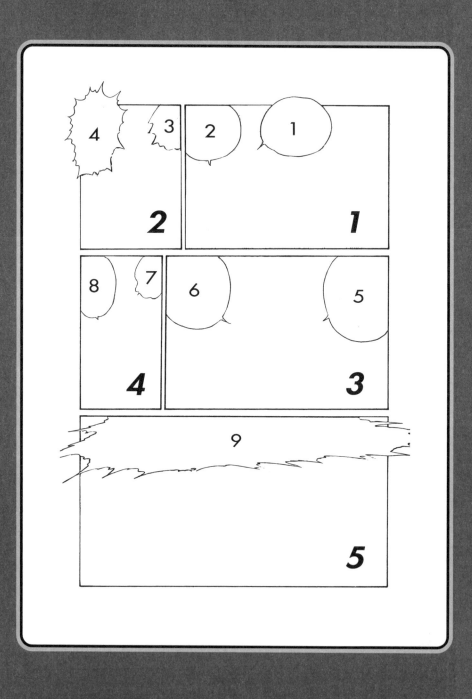

These sample pages from Eiichiro Oda's manga *One Piece* are presented in the Japanese reading order, from right to left.

Please enjoy this look behind the scenes of one of the most masterful manga of all time.

Pay attention to how he lays out his pages and the imagery or characters that he chooses to focus on. Put everything you've learned to use and study these pages!

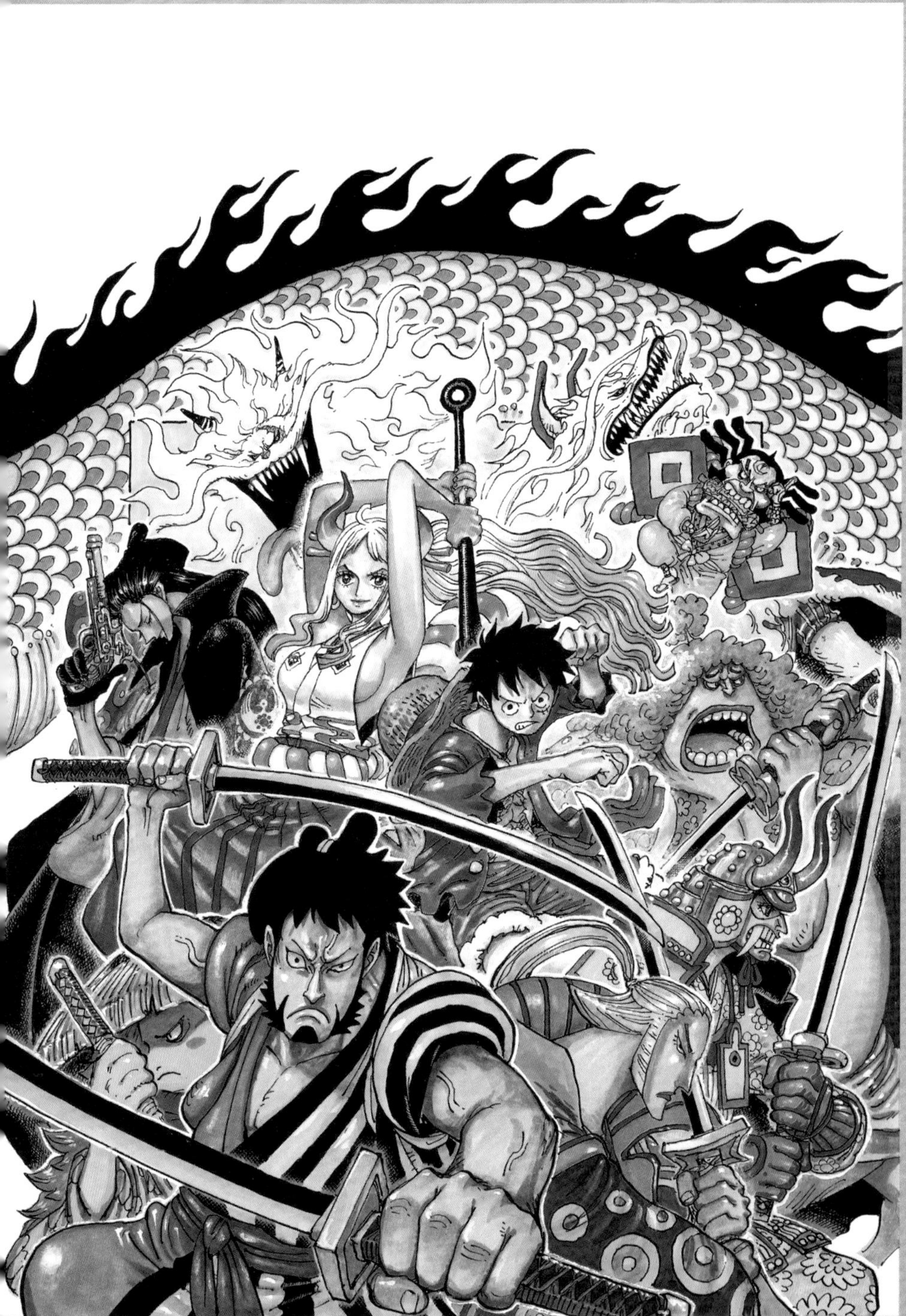

Volume 98 Cover

Hamlet's and Fourtricks's names don't appear on the draft since they were placed separately, by the designer, closer to the time of printing.

うわァ〜〜〜
"麦わら"と
ジンベエだ

めちゃ
くちゃ
強ェ!!
気をつけろ

城内
1階―

3
2
1

B1

B2

急げ
急げ!!!
錦えもんの
所へ!!!

とにかく
急げ!!!

おれだって
カイドウ
ぶっ飛ばし
てェんだ!!

"黒足"を
なぜ
言わねェ!!!

ダラしねェな
お前ら!!!

あァ!!

フォートリックス
様っ!!
ハムレット様!!
あいつら
止まらなくて!!

わあーあーあああ
よし もっかいだ!!!
アレ全部飛行能力者か?
ドド
ドドンッ!!
ウォオオ〜!!!
任せとけ――!!!
オオッ
オオッ

少年ジャンプ原稿
第40号
P. 83
コミックス
画稿修正
有・無

少年ジャンプ原稿

第45号

P. 82

コミックス
画秘密正

有・無

ママ〜〜ママ
ハハハ!!

調子にのんじゃねェよ!!
たかが数百人連れて来たくらいで!!

ム〜〜ハハハハ!!
全くだバカめ

プルルルル!!クイーン様!!

裏口より数千人の侵入者が城内へ!!!

え〜〜〜〜〜〜〜!!!

"花の都"で捕まった筈の侍達!!

兎丼の囚人達!!

先程の海賊達に元七武海ローも加わり全員が結託し勢いは増すばかり!!

更に入口よりなぜか!!
"不死鳥"マルコ"と
シャーロット・ペロスペロー!!

は——!?

バァン!!!

Having another border beyond panels that happen to cross the trim line makes it easier to understand for the art staff involved.

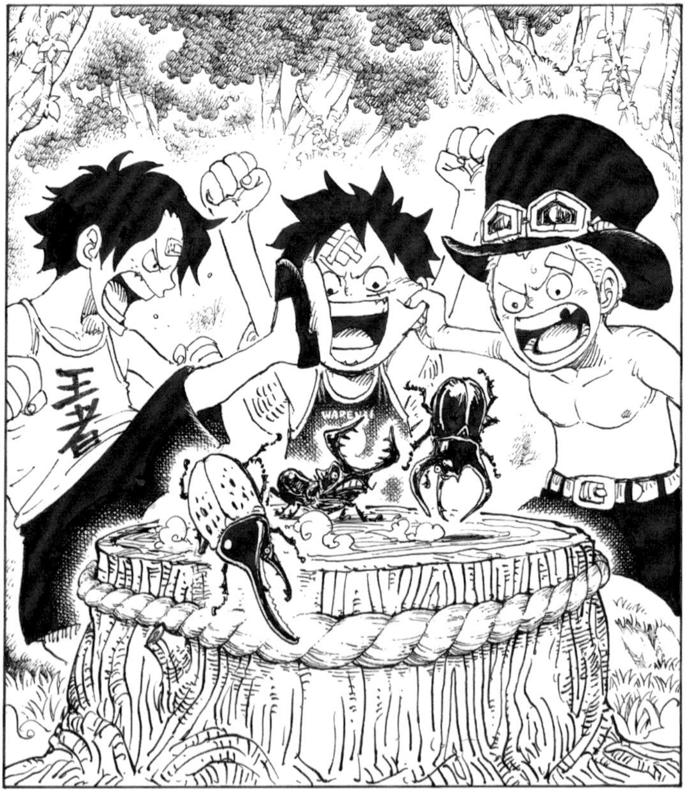
王者

少年ジャンプ原稿
第49号
P. 57
コミックス
画稿修正
有・無

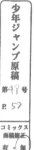